Three Essays,
1793–1795

Three Essays, 1793–1795

The Tübingen Essay,
Berne Fragments,
The Life of Jesus

by
G. W. F. HEGEL

*Edited and Translated
with Introduction and Notes by
Peter Fuss and John Dobbins*

University of Notre Dame Press
Notre Dame, Indiana

Library of Congress Cataloging in Publication Data

Hegel, Georg Wilhelm Friedrich, 1770–1831.
    Three essays, 1793–1795.

    Bibliography: p.
    Includes index.
    1. Jesus Christ—Biography—Addresses, essays,
lectures. 2. Christian biography—Palestine—Addresses,
essays, lectures. I. Fuss, Peter. II. Dobbins, John.
III. Title.
B2908 1984   193   83-40599
ISBN 0-268-01854-5

Contents

Preface

Until quite recently, Hegel's early writings have received scant attention in the English-speaking world. A notable exception was T. M. Knox's volume entitled *Early Theological Writings,* first published in 1948. It contained translations of selected material from Hermann Nohl's German edition of 1907, including "The Positivity of the Christian Religion" and "The Spirit of Christianity and its Fate." It also contained a lengthy introductory essay by Richard Kroner which treated the early writings only cursorily, being devoted for the most part to the tracing of germinal ideas developed more fully in Hegel's later work. Both scholars claimed, essentially without textual support, that Hegel's thought and sensibility underwent profound transformations between the time he left Tübingen Seminary in 1793 and the time he arrived in Jena in 1801. Not included among Knox's selections were what have since come to be known as the Tübingen Essay, the more interesting fragments from Hegel's Berne period, and the "Life of Jesus"—i.e. the subject-matter of the present volume. Following Nohl in treating the Tübingen and Berne essays as a continuous series of fragments, Knox discounted (in a way that Kroner did not) the importance of all three.[1]

Then, in 1972, H. S. Harris published his meticulous and searching study, *Hegel's Development: Toward the Sunlight, 1770–1801.* Professor Harris had carefully reexamined not only the early manuscripts but also the pioneering biographical and editorial work of Rosenkranz[2] and Haym, the later efforts of Dilthey, Nohl, Lasson, Rosenzweig, Glockner, Haering, and Hoffmeister, and the most recent contributions of Henrich, Lacorte, Peperzak, and Schüler (to mention only a few in each grouping). What Harris found characteristic throughout the period in question was a remarkable continuity of thought and purpose—modified, to be sure, but not nearly so radi-

1. "These have not seemed worth translation—the fragments because they are too fragmentary and are concerned in the main with questions treated more systematically and maturely in the essays which I have translated, the "Life of Jesus" because it is little more than a forced attempt to depict Jesus as a teacher of what is in substance Kant's ethics" (v).

2. Our bibliography provides further detail regarding authors and works mentioned here.

cally as had heretofore been claimed, after Hegel entered into the period of his maturity. In arriving at this conclusion, Harris took the
Tübingen Essay, the Berne fragments, and the "Life of Jesus" very
seriously, and even appended to his researches a literal translation of
most of the first work, and sprinkled his text liberally with excerpts
from the other two.

The present volume, then, may be taken as extending a little further what Knox began and Harris significantly furthered, even though
we disagree with Knox's evaluation and depart noticeably from Harris's method of translation. Of course, translation is unavoidably a
matter of compromises and trade-offs. Professor Harris, working from
Nohl rather than from the more recent Suhrkamp edition which (con-
servatively) normalizes Hegel's eccentric punctuation, aimed at absolute fidelity to the original. The result is a text that periodically bor-
ders on the unintelligible. Our primary aim in translating the essays
and fragments has been to produce texts that are as readable and conceptually coherent as the debatable limits of a translator's flexibility
will allow. We have repunctuated in order to break up Hegel's inter-
minable, run-on sentences (most of which end with a dash instead
of a period). We have paragraphed more frequently than Hegel, and
other writers of his time, were wont to do; and in several instances
we have paragraphed differently. On occasion we have altered the sequence of Hegel's phrasing so as to make the flow of the prose more
natural in English. We trust that Hegel himself would have counte-
nanced this much infidelity. In all other respects, we have done our
utmost to translate what we believe to be actually there. —We might
add that we found the Tübingen essay and the Berne fragments quite
difficult. One reason for this, we believe, is that whereas young Hegel
had indeed begun to think things through, he had by no means arrived at either a definitive conception or a precise mode of articula-
tion. The effects of Hegel's intellectual struggles in the 1790's are
reflected in the very structure of his sentences, whose already typical
convolutedness is accompanied by a formlessness that was soon to
become far less characteristic.

We do in any event urge our readers to consult Harris's translation
of the Tübingen essay (481–507) and the analysis he provides for it
(119–153), and for the Berne fragments (157–193), and for the "Life
of Jesus" (192–207). Also worthy of note is his chronological index
to Hegel's early writings (517–527). Although the brief interpreta-

tion that follows is our own and we alone are responsible for its short-comings, we are aware that we offer the knowledgeable Hegel scholar little more than one alternate and two fresh translations.

We owe special thanks to Professor Michael Washburn of Indiana University-South Bend for having initiated our involvement in this project, to Professor Henry Shapiro of the University of Missouri-St. Louis for having read portions of our manuscript with his understanding critical eye, and to Richard Allen, our editor at the Press, for his patience and encouragement.

Chronology of Hegel's Life and Career

1770   Born August 27 in Stuttgart, son of a civil servant for the Duchy of Württemberg (a stronghold of Swabian Protestantism in a predominantly Catholic portion of Germany).

1773   Birth of his sister Christiane, with whom he remained on close terms throughout his life.

1777   Enters Stuttgart Gymnasium and pursues classical studies.

1779   Lessing's *Nathan the Wise* published.

1781   Hegel's mother succumbs to fever.
Kant publishes his *Critique of Pure Reason.*

1785   Kant's *Foundations of the Metaphysics of Morals* published.

1788   Hegel graduates from the Gymnasium; is class valedictorian.
Enters University of Tübingen's theological seminary; studies philosophy and theology; forms close friendship with Hölderlin, subsequently with Schelling.
Kant's *Critique of Practical Reason* published.

1790   Earns Master of Philosophy degree.

1793   Drafts the Tübingen essay, passes his final examination in theology, and is engaged as a private tutor by a wealthy family in Berne, Switzerland, where he continues sketching various of his ideas concerning religion.
Kant's *Religion within the Limits of Reason Alone* published.

1794   Fichte publishes his *Wissenschaftslehre.*

1795   Hegel writes "The Life of Jesus" and "The Positivity of the Christian Religion."
Kant's *Perpetual Peace,* Schelling's *On the Ego* published.

1796   Hegel leaves Berne for a private tutorship in Frankfurt.

1797   Publication of Schelling's *Ideas for a Philosophy of Nature* and Hölderlin's *Hyperion.*

1798   Hegel begins drafting what has become known as "The Spirit of Christianity and Its Fate."
Fichte publishes his *System of Ethics;* is charged with atheism.

1799   Hegel's father dies, leaving him an inheritance sufficient for him to consider a university career.

1800   Fichte publishes *The Vocation of Man.*

1801   Hegel moves to Jena and soon begins university career as a lecturer; publishes *The Difference between Fichte's and Schelling's Systems.*

1802   Hegel and Schelling co-edit *The Critical Journal of Philosophy.*

1803   Hegel publishes *Faith and Knowledge* (a critique of Kant, Jacobi, and Fichte).

1804   Death of Kant.

1805   Promoted to associate professor; lectures on the history of philosophy; begins writing his *System of Science.*

1806   While Napoleon's armies are moving into Jena, Hegel completes the *Phenomenology of Spirit* (first part of his philosophical system).

1807   Fathers an illegitimate son (Ludwig) by the wife of his landlord; becomes newspaper editor in Bamberg. The *Phenomenology* is published.

1808   Becomes principal and philosophy professor at the Gymnasium in Nürnberg.
Fichte publishes *Addresses to the German Nation.*

1811   Is engaged to and marries Marie von Tücher.

1812   First child of his marriage, a girl, dies in infancy; his only brother, Ludwig, dies in Napoleon's Russian campaign.
Hegel publishes the first part of his *Logic.*

1813   Birth of son Karl.

1814   Birth of son Immanuel.

1816   Appointed professor at Heidelberg.
Second volume of the *Logic* is published.

1817   Son Ludwig joins family in Heidelberg.
Hegel publishes first version of the *Encyclopedia.*

1818   Accepts professorship at Berlin.

1821   *Philosophy of Right* is published.

1822   Begins several years of work on lectures on the philosophy of history, aesthetics, the philosophy of religion, and the history of philosophy.

1827   Revised and greatly expanded version of the *Encyclopedia* is published.

1829   Elected chancellor of the University of Berlin.

1831   Cholera epidemic in Berlin; Ludwig dies; Hegel himself dies.

1832   Christiane commits suicide.

Introduction

By the time that Hegel, then in his early twenties, was finishing his theological studies at Tübingen, Immanuel Kant's magisterial *Critique of Pure Reason* had begun to alter the form—and to some extent the content—of metaphysical and theological inquiry, even as its "Copernican turn" was providing the burgeoning empirical sciences with an ingenious rational foundation aimed at securing them from the more devastating skeptical implications of David Hume's radical empiricism. In this and in subsequent writings Kant seemed to have demonstrated conclusively that such matters of ultimate human concern as God, freedom, and immortality are not susceptible to rational proof or disproof. But although he was fully sympathetic with the Enlightenment's devotion to free rational inquiry and its contempt for religious superstition and political despotism, by "destroying knowledge in order to make room for faith" he had consciously broken with the main drift of its thought. In fact he was unwittingly inspiring a new wave of uses and abuses of reason among theologians—some claiming that Kant had emancipated religion from the standards of rationality altogether, others that his distinction between "theoretical" and "practical" reason could provide religion with a mode of conceptual respectability utterly different from that governing scientific inquiry.

Like his friends and classmates Schelling and Hölderlin, Hegel was at once a child of the Enlightenment, an avid reader of Kant, and a Romantic devotee of the humanism of the Athenian *polis;* and, at least initially, he responded with enthusiasm to the shibboleths of the French Revolution. But these young compatriots all had their doubts that rationalism—either in its extreme Enlightenment or even in its modified Kantian form—could answer to the religious and moral needs of the common people, to whom the voice of reason speaks most discernibly through the stirrings of the heart and the promptings of conscience. In this period Hegel was strongly drawn to the calling of a *Volkserzieher*—one who seeks to raise the moral consciousness of the populace at large by all the means at his disposal, not excluding artistic and mythopoeic devices. But unlike Schelling (five years Hegel's junior and something of a philosophical prodigy) and Hölderlin (who was already a poet, novelist, and dramatist of note before 1800), young Hegel experienced no early or meteoric rise to fame, and in fact would be well into his thirties before producing the sort of work for which he is best known. If he can be said to have persevered in anything during his student days, it was in his investigations (eclectic but assiduous and wide-reaching) of cultural history. Guided by these studies and by his own ripening philosophical instincts, Hegel was beginning to realize that, despite the efforts of Kant and others, the interconnections of reason, religion, and morality had become increasingly problematic for his era, both in theory and in practice. The unpublished drafts of 1793–94 contained here give us some indication of the lines of thought he was then pursuing; and his retelling of the story of Jesus in 1795 was evidently a first, largely experimental attempt to remedy the problem as he conceived it.

I. THE TÜBINGEN ESSAY (1793)

From the outset this incomplete and often labored draft sounds a recurrent critical theme: while a religious dimension is indispensable to and pervasive in human experience, the religion that predominates in our culture responds to the deeper human needs inadequately and inconsistently. While Christianity's purest leaven—which consists of a few basic and universal moral principles everyone can understand and assent to in good conscience, along with faith in a wise and benevolent deity who is eternally just and merciful—reinforces what we intuitively know and feel, much of Christian theological doctrine, ritual, and ceremony is irrational, despiriting, and degrading. Much of Christian religious experience and practice is an agonized counterpoint between bouts of sensuous indulgence and a self-hatred grounded in an abstract and unattainable ideal of perfection and purity. This matter-spirit dualism had of late been exacerbated in philosophical quarters by the ethical purism of Kant, which made it seem as if "heteronomous" and "autonomous" wills—and truly moral action as distinguished from merely prudential conduct—were articulating two entirely distinct worlds. While Hegel at this point in his thinking is willing to grant that such distinctions may be valid on purely abstract, theoretical grounds, he is convinced that they have served to deflect the Christian mentality even further from a realistic appreciation of the sensuous and pragmatic context in which our rational and moral capacities have to find their fulfillment. Even at the age of twenty-three Hegel is not far from insisting that reason, the rose in the cross of the present, must demonstrate its genius precisely in its power to actualize itself in the mundane without simply bypassing or transcending it.

To be sure, religion has always been more than a mere body of arcane, otherworldly dogma. Traditionally it seeks to move the heart, influence the feelings, and draw the will out of its preoccupation with baser, pettier, and merely private affairs, toward higher moral and rational ends. But this quite legitimate function has been to a large extent compromised and even perverted by religion's monumental endeavor to objectify itself in the minds and understanding of men. Hegel maintains, nonetheless, that everything depends on how our hearts and sensibilities are disposed, how receptive these are to higher ends, especially the moral. What is needed to restore the subjective vitality of religion is that it be genuinely humanized, that it be a *Volksreligion* addressing the many-tiered needs and aspirations of an entire people in an integrated and cohesive fashion — one that, while of course allowing for special, private counsel for the individual in his particular situation, is primarily concerned with the animation of a universal spirit.

Accordingly, Hegel is skeptical that any improvement of the understanding of men, even if gradually feasible, will accomplish much in the intended direction. Although such efforts might facilitate the codification of moral principles and rules of moral casuistry, the fact remains that the understanding is not an effective force in the moment of morally significant action. Beyond this, even if the few truths which we do seem universally to acknowledge were to be articulated "in their purity as reason demands," they would be so out of keeping with everyday sensuous experience that few men could ever hope to take them to heart in this form; and the few that do would comprise only an isolated spiritual elite who, while themselves liberated from the need of cruder forms of religious edification, invite charges of hypocrisy and authoritarian manipulation whenever they try to "improve" their less enlightened brethren. Indeed the relative airiness of such efforts is readily observable in the tendency of men to return, when next they find themselves in difficulty, to the tried and true ways of religious sentiment, superstitious or otherwise. —What is really wanted is not enlightened, ratiocinative scientificality, but a truly practical wisdom which can speak to the mass of humanity in such way as to enlarge its vision, ennoble its feelings, and enhance its sense of autonomy and self-worth.

But we must not misunderstand Hegel's standpoint here. Despite the tendency of the men of the Enlightenment to attack "idolatrous" popular religion with intellectualistic abstractions and reductivistic arguments, its own heart was animated by an ideal that is in fact Hegel's as well. The problem is simply that a universal church of the rational spirit is and remains a mere ideal of reason. For the most part, Hegel seems prepared to settle for a public whose tendency to fetishism and sense-bound self-comprehension is minimized by a functional, communicative religion urging them toward greater rationality.

But even this rather modest endeavor may prove futile if much weight is given to one objection to Kant's moral perfectionism, namely that unless we are able to identify empirically some sort of moral impulse somewhere within the economy of human nature, we should admit that we really have no sense of what it might mean for us to be moral agents at all. Apparently Hegel thought that he could reply to this objection in a way that Kant could not. He maintains that there are quasi-moral sentiments interwoven into empirical human nature. Although these lack the consistency of law-bound actions and the inherent moral goodness (hence worthiness of respect) of purely moral principles of conduct, they nonetheless curb our baser inclinations and help elicit what is best in us (thereby meriting encouragement). Included here are all of our more benign impulses: good will, compassion, amicability, etc. Furthermore, our empirical character, even though hemmed in by natural inclinations, includes something which is at least germinally a true moral sentiment—namely love, specifically that non-selfcentered love which has a certain affinity with the concerned disinterestedness characteristic of reason in its highest manifestations. —It is worth noting here that Hegel not only never repudiated this conception of the human capacity for love, but subsequently developed it further.

Still, young Hegel is disinclined to take very much for granted regarding human nature. Precisely because "man is such a many-sided creature that anything can be made of him," Hegel thinks it necessary that there must be a religious force designed to sustain the high ideals of moral and political virtue, lest humanity end up squandering itself on base and slavish practices.

With this in mind Hegel began sketching plans and experimenting with various ways of articulating what would need to be done (a task that would dominate his reflection and writing for the next five or so years), and the present essay sets forth several of the criteria of a more humanized religion. The doctrines of such a religion must have their source and sanction in reason—the kind of universal reason to which the heart and conscience can relate and give ready assent. These must be simple, few in number, comprehensible without elaborate rational demonstration, and practicable without a sophisticated casuistry of qualifications and exceptions. In their form they must be tailored to the specific moral level of consciousness attained within the culture for which they are designed—and this may very well require a compromising of some of their ideal rational purity. In this matter our overindoctrinated and bogey-ridden Christian religiosity may very well embarrass us when compared with the rational and moral simplicity of, say, ancient Greek faith.

With regard to the customs and practices essential to such a religion, they are preferably derived from the spirit of the people themselves; otherwise they tend to be artificial impositions. In certain respects our Christian rites of propitiation and atonement, for instance, are barbarous—involving a kind of compulsive mortifying of the flesh and self-abasement of the spirit that no heathen would have been capable of—and compare quite poorly with the more natural spirit of gratitude displayed in Greek sacrifice.

Lastly, it is clear that the contemplated religion must be one that unobtrusively and constructively blends with the needs and interests of everyday life even while it performs the essential function of rallying our higher impulses and motivations to action in this very context. Again, in contrast with the folk festivals of the ancient Greeks, which accomplished this very well, our Christian religion browbeats the communicant into regarding all worldly concerns as vain distractions from the demands of the spirit even while the collection basket is being passed. After reemphasizing the natural interplay between a nonalienating civil religion and the enhancement of the political virtues, notably freedom, self-confidence, and self-reliance, the Tübingen essay breaks off with an experiment (quickly abandoned) in florid cross-cultural allegory designed to make ideologues of Christian progressivism squirm.

II. RELATED FRAGMENTS
FROM THE BERNE PERIOD (1793–94)

Difficult as it may be to date and to sort out the extant fragments from this period, they give evidence of being conceptually more advanced than the Tübingen essay. The first of the fragments we have translated (Nohl 30–32) should quickly dispel any illusion that young Hegel might have naively relished the idea of donning the mantle of public educator. He knew too well what was at stake. In a world such as ours, a would-be *Volkserzieher* really has no *Volk* to address. Screened from the world at large by a veil of anonymity, he may vent the force of his moral frustrations with a ferocity he would never direct at those he knows personally, especially those who share his sense of prevailing corruptness and yet hear a call to higher aspirations that refuses to be silenced. Indeed from the public (whose attention he cannot get without exaggeration and oversimplification, yet to whom he must speak from his own experience since this is all he knows) he expects some magical transformation and improvement. He is, in short, a hypocrite and a daydreamer. But what are his options? Neither Greek moral urbanity (Hegel is still nostalgic for it, but sees no hope of its resurrection) nor Jewish moral vituperation (were such even desirable) would find a viable context in our society. Self-perfection seems as plausible an ideal as it ever has, although by now its relation to the common weal has become endlessly complicated. If antiquity already had its moral isolates, how much more alluring—and impossible—must this choice appear today. Perhaps the most seductive course is the one that turns out to be no solution at all: the Roman objectification of virtue, the subservience of everything individual (even decision-making) to an all-encompassing Will of the State—something we in the West came to know again a century after Hegel's death in the grotesquely caricatured form of totalitarianism.

The dilemma young Hegel was facing at this point may well have been pivotal in the story of his own development. What is to be his stance when, as member of a modern, morally decadent society, he means to initiate cultural reform? Deriving little inspiration from among his contemporaries, he looks to antiquity for exemplary moral heroes. These he finds—and in the process learns how differently each had to cope with his distinctive culture. Socrates worked from within, appealing to the higher-minded. Diogenes dropped out. The Romans, prior to their degeneration, somehow subjugated the complex passions of the individual to the persona of the staunch citizen. And neither Jesus in his own person nor the religion bearing his name ever resolved the conflict between the universality and the exclusivity expressed in the spiritual aspirations and demands they insisted upon. —But in any event Hegel's culture is not theirs, and no model from a bygone age can be fruitfully imitated. The very fabric of religion and morals in his culture is defective. So where to turn and what to do?

The eventual solution for Hegel was, of course, "the rational is the actual," etc.[1] But in 1793 Hegel hadn't really got that far. True, reason and the life of rationality was already his ideal. But this was precisely the problem. It was intransigently ideal, balking at every attempt to instantiate it in the real world. Within little more than a decade the decisive breakthrough will have occurred: the rational is not a matter of ideal *versus* real at all, but is the reality of the real, the actual, itself. This will be Hegel's philosophical reinterpretation of the Christian "Word made flesh"—whatever Christianity may choose to think of it. The 1806 *Phenomenology* is the *Commedia* of the modern age, the experimental and experiential working-through of his newfound concept. The simple but giant step not yet taken in the 1790's is: We don't really need more reformers and reform schemes (although these are necessarily and rightly always with us); we need to comprehend what is, for within it both the means and the imperative are already, if latently, present. —But here in 1793–94 we are with a younger Hegel who is frustrated and perplexed, but persistent. He starts one draft after another, trying at least to get his problem clear; and no satisfying resolution is as yet in sight. He stops again and again in midstream, sometimes in midsentence, lacking the surehandedness which only a resolution of his perplexity could provide.

In the second fragment (Nohl 32–35), Hegel is again contrasting— with a vehemence typical only of this period of his life—the humanism of the Greeks with the sectarian and authoritarian atmosphere surrounding Gospel Christianity. Nathanael, Joseph of Arimathea,

---

1. See in particular his preface to the *Philosophy of Right* (and his astute evaluation of Plato's *Republic* there).

and Nicodemus are perhaps the only ones who might have been fit companions for a Socrates. Understandably, their loftiness of spirit, independence of mind, and lack of susceptibility to mystification made them quite unfit for the yoke of discipleship.

The argument of the third fragment (Nohl 36–39) sounds a little like an early draft of part of Freud's *Civilization and its Discontents*. Much of primitive antiquity was characterized by an "ethical simplicity" long since lost in Western civilization, which ever since the first flowerings of the Christian soul has been beset by a "divided consciousness." The relentless advance of reason, culminating in the Enlightenment's rationalistic assault on all manner of faith, feeling, and sentiment (as merely atavistic tendencies), has not cut deep enough to remake human nature in its image. Hence the modern-day enlightened and sophisticated Christian: skeptical of and embarrassed by his own faith, nostalgic for the unity and integrity of some alleged past, and full of feelings incompatible with a ratiocinative intellect which keeps forcing them into repressed and displaced modes of survival.

But there is something else discernible here. Hegel's prose is so markedly convoluted not because he cannot write more clearly (specimens from before and after, including "The Life of Jesus," show that he can) but because his reflections on the project at hand — to revitalize popular morale and morality through the instrumentality of a civil religion — are clouded by self-doubt. The endless qualifications and misgivings, the labored attempt at even-handedness as he weighs the pros and cons of other epochs against his own, the impasse he reaches regarding how to implement his program: all these testify to an interesting and challenging undertaking which young Hegel ("the old man," as his intimates called him) nonetheless progressively sees through — and eventually beyond. When (e.g. Nohl 38) he accuses his own age of confusing the disappearance of ancient ethical simplicity with the demise of morality as such, he is anticipating, though he is hardly aware of it, the radically altered perspective of the *Phenomenology* and the other works of his maturity. And this if only for a simple but striking fact that appears to have eluded his contemporaries: for all of the corruptness and decadence of the modern age, modern society survives its recurrent crises whereas those older ones we tend to romanticize succumbed to theirs. This phenomenon is what he presently undertook to unravel; indeed his life's work could be said to be that undertaking. Hegel's identification of the rational with the actual, his reconciliation of what ought to be with what is, became the faith, the foundation, and the telos of his mature thought.

The fourth fragment (Nohl 39–42) contains unmistakable echoes-in-advance of the *Phenomenology*'s famous "Struggle of Enlightenment with Superstition" (Chapter VI, B, ii, a.). But the balance characteristic of Hegel's later dialectic is not sustained here; he quickly reverts to an independent critical assessment of Gospel Christianity's shortcomings as a prospective candidate for the office of civil religion.

In the fifth fragment (Nohl 42–44), the spotlight is mainly on the Reformation. Hegel is quite critical of its guiding spirits, although there is a faint undercurrent of sympathy with their plight. Longing for the unity, purity, and simplicity of an authentic Christian *Volksreligion* (which in fact never existed, Christianity having emerged from the catacombs only to become an imperial protégé and then an imperium in its own right), they had a predilection for the extreme disciplines appropriate only for small groups of relatively high-minded individuals, even while igniting the religious and cultural tinder of a whole continent. But a monastic/"masonic" regimen at the foundation of a supposed *Volksreligion* in the modern age is a formula for reform hardly promising much success. Hegel reiterates his conviction that the universally valid core of religious experience is what is commonly expressed as (and in) improving the heart, repentance, and conversion. When conventional religion stops at that, it is being prudent—rather like the law when it confines itself to legally established guilt, without pretending competence in probing the soul of the accused. Christian reformers, however, have never known such restraint. In these passages we find a preview, both in content and in tone, of Nietzsche's anti-Christian diatribes. Almost a century earlier, young Hegel had recognized that Christianity had unleashed something momentous and irreversible. However frequently the upshot may thus far have been neurosis and compulsivity, Holy Mother Church has undeniably activated in her faithful a capacity for introspection heretofore unknown. This recognition was to become the guiding theme of *Phenomenology,* Chapter IV, B: the maturation of a sense of self amidst the travails of the "Unhappy Consciousness."

The end of the sixth fragment (Nohl 44–45) intensifies Hegel's perplexity as to how a civil religion might be effectuated. Its core must be morality. But morality cannot be instituted as can, say, the law. And the populace at large is not well disposed toward custodians of public morality.

The seventh fragment (Nohl 45–47: one of the few to which Hegel himself gave a title) may well be the most crucial in this series, for it strikes at the heart of conventional Christianity as candidate for Hegel's ideal of a viable civil religion. In theory, the Christian's faith in eternal salvation, which he conceives as an afterlife, is supposed to render him indifferent to the joys and miseries of his earthly life, including its natural terminus, death. In practice, the fear that his afterlife may well be one of lengthy purgation (for wrongdoings in this life) or even eternal damnation (either as punishment or as a preordained fate) torments the Christian's daily life and terrorizes him in his hour of death. The result is radical alienation from the life process itself—an estrangement that young Hegel, at least, seems to regard not as the crucible of spiritual growth but rather as the breeding ground of emotional hysteria and wholesale demoralization.

Of course Hegel's later assessment of Christianity is much more ambivalent and far less given to nostalgic and invidious comparisons of it with even more ancient forms of religion. Underlying this modification of attitude was the discovery that Christian theology could be translated into the conceptual language of his own pan-reconciliatory dialectic. But, although he obviously became more patient with it, there is no evidence that he became any less critical of the kind of mentality he attacked and satirized in these fragments.

Most noteworthy in the eighth fragment (Nohl 48–50) are its first three paragraphs. Taken together, their argument is that religious experience (as distinguished from erudition, the keeping up of appearances, etc.) consists essentially in a strong disposition to moral virtue, animated by the idea of an all-encompassing—and to this extent transcendent—telos.

The second paragraph of the ninth fragment (Nohl 50–60) again suggests, this time more overtly, that "the idea of God" is to be understood as expressive of mankind's species-defining sense of a moral purpose for its existence that transcends all ephemeral preoccupations (anticipating, in content and form, the dialectic of Enlightenment in Chapter VI, B of the *Phenomenology*). Of particular interest is the paragraph that follows. If Hegel's footnote is more than a polite concession to establishment mentality, it may well preview his lifelong effort to articulate the enduring conceptual truth he found in Christianity —an effort that turned out to involve such complexity of thought and difficulty of expression that, in light of his own criteria, it could scarcely have been enlisted in the service of a civil religion.

Hegel proceeds here to test Christianity as we have come to know and practice it against the criteria he has set forth (at Nohl 20) for a desirable civil religion. By each of them Christianity fails. A religion given to "arcane, incomprehensible dogmas" is an affront to universal reason, not one whose teachings are founded thereon. Were it to consist entirely of such dogmas, the imagination, the heart, and the senses would indeed "go away empty-handed in the process" — as would the memory, left with words to recite but nothing of substance to retain. A religion so constituted would hardly be such "that all of life's needs, including public and official transactions, would be bound up with it." But of course Christianity is even more an elaborate edifice of practices (secular and symbolically transcendent, aesthetic and ascetic) than it is a body of obscure and alien dogmas. These practices, many of them morally reprehensible, certainly do engage our several faculties and address life's needs — for better and for worse. Hegel's descriptions of how Christian practices can inflame the imagination, corrupt the heart, and derange the senses might well have been penned (no doubt more eloquently) by a Voltaire. Thus it may come as a bit of a surprise to find Hegel preferring Jesus to Socrates as humankind's ideal spiritual prototype precisely because of his human-transcending yet incarnated nature.[2] But Hegel promptly adds (Nohl 58) that the tension between what one is and what one ideally might be constructively animates only a very small portion of our species; the vast majority, though by no means oblivious to transcendent demands, have a way of disfiguring the image and distorting the message of the original which their faith bids them to imitate. Once again, therefore, we are left without any realistic prospect for a truly civil religion. The remainder of the fragment (Nohl 59–60) resumes the assault on Christendom's defects, notably the moral hypocrisy of its missionary zeal, whose first manifestation Hegel detects in the facile way in which the Apostles made converts.

The tenth fragment (Nohl 60–69) opens with more invective against

---

2. (See Nohl 57.) The reader should note that Hegel here once again reaffirms the need of the human heart and imagination for loftier-than-human ideals, however much an epistemologically fettered "Kantian understanding" might fall short of cognitive access to such ideals. There is little merit in the claim that Hegel only "discovered" the heart and its legitimate demands some five or so years later, and that he was through and through a Kantian rationalist (was Kant?) in 1793.

the contemporary Christian establishment's "scandalous" modes of representing spiritual requirements to the faithful, who in turn, skeptical though they may be, are not inclined to sustained rebelliousness in religious matters. After yet another of his frequent and not very impressive attempts at marshalling his material (doctrines, traditions, ceremonies), Hegel returns to the lists, this time to point out the incompatibility between reason's teaching that a human life devoted to virtue and reflection is its own reward—and Christianity's freedom-denying doctrine that Original Sin precludes our being truly good, and that genuine happiness is to be found only in an afterlife, where it is dispensed in seemingly arbitrary fashion by the grace of God. Before he has finished this line of argument, Hegel has introduced yet another, namely that even the more concrete aspect of Christian doctrine, namely the historical actuality of Christ, when made into an article of faith (and belief in it a condition of salvation), once again outrages reason and moral common sense because of its esoteric, authoritarian, and exclusionary character. But perhaps the most striking moment in this section is a positive one: Hegel's insistence (Nohl 67) that our species has demonstrated a capacity for moral dignity far beyond what Christian dogma will grant. And it may well be that Hegel already had in mind to do something like "The Life of Jesus" so as to provide his own answer to the question he asks at this point (Nohl 68): "By what arrangements could it be brought to pass that in Christ not just a human being, not merely his name, but virtue itself be known and loved?"

On the face of it the concluding fragment (Nohl 70–71), with its rapid shift in mood from civic despair to moral optimism, seems to do little more than faithfully reflect the conflicting emotions of a disillusioned but inveterately idealistic youth. To leave it at that, however, will not do. Neither at Tübingen nor in Berne did Hegel manage to find or invent a viable civil religion for his time. But its ideal, as he conceived this, had achieved a measure of historical actualization in the past and continued to hold some prospect for realization in the future. For all that he essentially demanded was that such a religion be based on the highest moral principles within the reach of the human spirit, that its practices encourage our minds to rise above the merely sensuous and ephemeral, and that the application of its doctrines foster a social and political climate in which individuals are conscious of their freedom, dignity, and mutual responsibility. —Hegel invites us to ponder one more invidious distinction. Despite its undeniable chauvinism and limited moral vision, the republic of classical antiquity did basically qualify as a civil religion. By contrast, Christendom's religious alienation, sense-bound morality, and relegation of political responsibility to despots is—especially in view of the long time it has had to mature and develop—a world-historical outrage. So much by way of grounds for despair.

But young Hegel is, after all, Hegel. The rose in the cross of the present—the flower that two millennia of Christendom has, in spite of everything, done a good deal to nurture—is already discernible to him. It is the long-developing idea of the moral person, of a being whose autonomous recognition of his infinite spiritual worth may one day make him less susceptible to institutions that seek to dehumanize, as well as to the psychology of desperation latent in all forms of otherworldliness.

III. "THE LIFE OF JESUS" (1795)

The abortive ending of the Tübingen essay gives us a hint as to why Hegel went to the trouble of retelling the story of Jesus at all. Graeco-phile and unsparing critic of Christianity that he was at this time, Hegel must have dreamt occasionally of a Hellenic folk religion in modern garb. But there was no way to translate such a dream into reality; and there was every reason to suppose that Christianity was here to stay. If Christianity (or for that matter any other religion) had little chance of becoming a folk religion in the modern age, it might nonetheless be induced to approximate more closely than it had in the past to a religion of reason and virtue. Hence what could be more natural than for Hegel to portray Jesus, its founder, as an apostle of reason and virtue—and of little else? Throughout his essay Hegel clearly plays down the role of Jesus as prophet and miracle-worker—indeed at one point he construes a "miracle" as a simple act of kindness (Nohl 88). And if the authoritarian mentality of his audience required Jesus to claim divine authority just to be heard, Hegel nevertheless has him steadfastly refusing to claim it for his own person or to impose such an idea on others in any way.

Even then, of course, the task facing Jesus was formidable. Teacher of a religion of morality, freedom, reason, and the promptings of the heart, he confronted a society that at worst tended to be mean-spirited, authoritarian, self-rationalizing, and contemptuous of inner feeling. And at its very best its concept of morality and moral purpose—ironically, in a way that anticipates the central and most vexing failure of Christendom—is thoroughly sense-bound and caught up in irrelevant subspiritual practices. Most interesting is Hegel's apparent intention to arouse the self-consciousness of the Christian sensibility by having Jesus, who is anything but ascetic, censure in God's chosen people the very fault which the Christian believes himself to be above, and which in actual fact is his most characteristic failing: his entire concept of divine purpose, spirituality, and the transcendence of sense is itself almost entirely sense-bound and preoccupied with irrelevant concerns. Thus Hegel's Jesus not only feels alienated from his own people, but would feel equally if not more so in Christian Europe—hardly an encouraging assessment of modern Christendom.

A few remarks may be in order concerning the alleged "Kantian cast" of this essay. There is no denying that the language of "The Life of Jesus" frequently brings to mind Kantian terms and considerations. But to make much of this fact may be to get things backward. Kant himself tended to couch his moral philosophy—which he took to be articulating a universally human rather than a sectarian point of view—in language often reminiscent of the Bible. Regarding more substantive matters, the essay's opening sentence ("Pure reason, transcending all limits, is divinity itself—whereby and in accordance with which the very plan of the world is ordered.") is not only a speculative proposition concerning the principle of divinity that Hegel could well have written at any point in his career; it also contains a germinal implication that anticipates the central component of his later concept of human spiritual endeavor. One might tend to think of the deity as abiding in transcendent, passive, static isolation; but such a notion fails to comprehend the very principle of divinity, which entails the active transcending of limits. This same principle, active in human thinking and rational endeavor, reveals itself in the world through our rational capacity to think beyond and indeed to go beyond the limits initially set for us by nature and the artificial limits imposed upon us by our own caprice, obstinacy, and malice. The early exhortations of Jesus invoke a rational faculty capable as such of moving one towards moral and spiritual perfection. No such faculty is to be found in Kant's *Critique of Pure Reason,* and even the Kantian "practical reason" lacks the power that Hegel attributes to reason

here. Moreover, it is obvious not only that for Hegel the moral substance of the Gospel story is the overriding issue, but that what is
of lasting value in the New Testament even today is the moral and
rational personhood of Jesus—something that he shares in common
with other paragons of our species, some of whom were not Christians. As Hegel's careful restructuring and rewording of one episode
after another makes abundantly clear, his Jesus is meant to be a universal representative of universally valid truths. From Hegel's own
point of view, he is not so much Kantianizing the New Testament
as debarbarizing it.

Much has been written about the influences, apart from Kant, on
Hegel's thinking during his formative years; and we urge our readers
to consult Harris, etc. for extensive efforts to trace them. But we
would be remiss if we did not mention Jean-Jacques Rousseau, who
had a decisive influence not only on young Hegel himself but on several generations of Hegel's countrymen. Perhaps the force of Rousseau's impact can best be appreciated by quoting him directly. At the
beginning of the Tübingen essay Hegel has a rather ambivalent depiction of prayer. Rousseau had written:

> . . . I practice contemplating the sublime. I meditate on the
> order of the universe, not so as to try to explain it by means
> of vain systems, but to admire it unceasingly, to worship the
> wise author who makes his presence felt in it. . . . But I do
> not pray to him. What would I ask of him? To change the
> course of things for my sake? To perform miracles on my
> behalf? . . . Nor do I ask him for the power to do good: why
> ask him for what he has already given me? Has he not given
> me conscience for loving the good, reason for knowing it, and
> freedom for choosing it? If I do evil, I have no excuse; I do
> it because I want to. Asking him to change my will is to ask
> of him what he asks of me; it is wanting him to do my work
> while I collect the wages for it. . . .³

Regarding the distinction—central to all the work of Hegel translated here—between a "natural" religion of reason, feeling, and vir-

---

3. *Emile,* Book IV (Paris: Garnier Frères, 1964, pp. 358–9). The translation above
is our own. The best English translation currently available is by Allan Bloom (New
York: Basic Books, 1979, pp. 293–4).

tue and an institutionalized "revealed" religion of positive doctrines
and dogmas, Rousseau had had this to say:

> You see in my exposition nothing but natural religion; how
> strange that any other is needed! . . . Of what can I possibly
> be guilty if I serve God in keeping with such insight as he gives
> my mind and the feelings he inspires in my heart? . . . The
> noblest ideas of divinity come to us from reason alone. Behold
> the spectacle of nature, listen to the inner voice. Hasn't God
> said everything to our eyes, to our conscience, to our judgment?
> What more is there for men to tell us? Their revelations, by
> giving God human passions, serve only to degrade him. Instead
> of clarifying our notions of the great Being, particular dogmas
> confuse them. . . . To the inconceivable mysteries surrounding
> him, they add absurd contradictions. They make man proud,
> intolerant, cruel. And rather than establishing peace on earth,
> they bring to it fire and the sword. . . .
>
> I am told that a revelation was needed to teach men the manner
> in which God wanted to be served. By way of proof one cites
> the diversity of bizarre forms of worship men have instituted;
> one fails to see that this very diversity comes from the capri-
> ciousness of revelations. So soon as various peoples presumed
> to make God speak, each made him speak after its own fashion
> and make him say what it wished. Had one listened solely to
> what God says to a man's heart, there would never have been
> more than one religion on earth.[4]

And as for Hegel's later, somewhat more reconciliatory attitude toward the Christian faith, Rousseau's words to a correspondent in 1763
seem apropos: "True Christianity is nothing but natural religion explained better."[5]

IV. HEGEL'S LATER PHILOSOPHY OF RELIGION

Regardless of one's critical standpoint, Hegel's mature philosophical
system can scarcely be viewed as lacking in audacity. It purports to

---

4. Ibid., p. 361 (Bloom p. 295). In both of the passages just quoted, it is the
Savoyard vicar speaking; but there is little reason to doubt that he is speaking for
Rousseau.

5. *Emile*, Garnier edition, p. 625, note 145.

articulate nothing short of "the true in the form of the true" and in so doing to complement and complete the many intellectual efforts that have striven to comprehend truth without adequately elaborating it in its true form. What is this truth? In one word: spirit. This is what Hegel conceives as the innermost principle of movement and potential informing the human world in every coherent, intelligible, and purposive manifestation. Of course, stating the matter in such abstract terms accomplishes little. The workings of spirit as it concretizes itself must be meticulously charted by a mind that not only enters into its seemingly inexhaustible finite manifestations without losing sight of their underlying thread of meaning and unity (the aim of phenomenology), but comprehends the essential nature of spirit, the structure of its potential and modes of actualization (the task of logic). Hegel took up this thread by evaluating the philosophical conceptualizations of earlier ages, noting the gradual evolution that resulted from the interplay between the constructive and the critical capacities he finds inherent in each. In this way he arrived at the critical standpoint from which he worked out his philosophy of mind, nature, history, aesthetics, the *polis,* and religion—the whole system of the human spirit's endeavors comprehended from within, on its own terms, and by the light of its own deepening self-consciousness. And the only modification he makes of the claim that his efforts yield the true in the form of the true is his insistence in addition that philosophy invents nothing, that it merely (!) thinks the actual through in its essential entirety.

Our focus here will be primarily on the lectures on the philosophy of religion that Hegel gave in Berlin between 1821 and 1831, the last decade of his life. Although he did not publish these either, they have been reconstructed and published since on the basis of his own manuscripts and several approximately verbatim student notebooks.[6] Hegel dedicated these lectures to the restoration of serious interest in knowing God—something of which he finds his age to have largely de-

---

6. The title of the currently most accessible German text, and the one which we have used here as the basis of our own translations, is *Vorlesungen über die Philosophie der Religion,* Hamburg: Felix Meiner, 1974 (in two volumes and four parts, each independently paginated). Our citations to this edition will appear directly in the body of our discussion and will identify volume, part, and page. We regret that the new critical edition of these lectures is not yet in print. The one English-language edition thus far available is *Lectures on Philosophy of Religion,* translated by E. B. Spiers and J. B. Sanderson (three volumes), New York: Humanities Press, 1962. For one of the most recent studies of Hegel's philosophy of religion, including

spaired. "The more the knowledge of finite things has spread thanks to the almost boundless expansion of the [empirical] sciences . . .the more has the sphere of the knowledge of God narrowed" (I,I,4). In his introduction, Hegel defines religion as "consciousness of [our] connectedness with God," and religion's object as "that which is sheerly unconditioned, utterly sufficient, existing for its own sake, — the absolute beginning and end-purpose in and of itself" (I,I,7). This "absolute content" is also the object of philosophy of religion, as it had heretofore been the object of academic metaphysics or natural theology. The latter, however, was a product of the formalistic understanding, whereas Hegel's intention is to conceive God speculatively, by means of dialectical reason, and as spirit (I,I,7–8). In his own day, Hegel finds rampant a kind of "cultivated reflection" which has no patience for a sympathetic critical examination of religious experience, and pitted against it a residue of traditional religious sentiment which is justifiably suspicious of this brand of sophisticated ratiocination although it itself lacks "the courage of knowledge, of truth and freedom" (I,I,25–8). The result is a religious sensibility that is needlessly on the defensive, an understanding that is shallow and inadequately grounded, and a skepticism that takes upon itself to dictate the course and pace of all inquiry. Hegel's goal is to remedy this by deepening our comprehension of the nature of reality and vindicating religion's legitimate demands and aspirations; only in this way is skepticism to be deprived of the main source of its plausibility.

Adequately comprehended in philosophical conceptualization, religious doctrine is spirit's most impressive form of self-articulation, just as communal religious worship evokes spirit's living presence among men. Because it is of the essence of spirit to concretize itself, systematic study of religion requires the most careful attention to the various manifestations of the religious spirit in the subjective consciousness of successive generations. But Hegel is equally insistent that any religion worthy of the name "is a product of the divine spirit, not an invention of man . . ." (I, I,44). Spirit's reality and truth is in fact to be found neither in an abstracted God nor in un-

---

copious references to his other texts, see James Yerkes, *The Christology of Hegel,* Albany: State University of New York Press, 1983. In our judgment, Yerkes overstates Hegel's religious orthodoxy, and his first chapter, on Hegel's early writings, suffers in comparison with Harris's interpretation.

mediated human feelings and yearnings. Moreover — and this too Hegel directs against his contemporaries — faith and reason cannot really exist bifurcated, irreconcilably opposed, or even merely indifferent to one another. "The human spirit in its innermost essence is not something thus divided, in which two [such capacities] in contradiction with one another could persist" (I,I,55). In their higher and purer forms, religion and philosophy are both ways of worshipping (or celebrating or serving: *Gottesdienst* connotes all three) God (I,I,29).

The method Hegel proposes consists of loosely following the historical unfolding of the central content of religious consciousness. As he examines each of the great world religions, he first analyses its representation of the world and man's highest strivings. In each case its own initial concept is found to be incapable of providing an adequate account of what ultimately underlies its own endeavors. However capable of touching or eliciting a substantial impetus within the soul, each of these representations is found to be too sense-bound and hence abstractly out of touch with its own ground and *telos;* each falls short of adequate conceptualization. But once he has arrived at Christianity, Hegel finds a religion whose central content and distinctive concept is adequately comprehensive and self-articulating, regardless of the representational monsters it may generate peripherally when miscomprehended. As such it qualifies as an "absolute religion," i.e. religion that is essentially free of fixated preoccupations with one-sided determinations and representations. Here for the first time the stage is set for a truly "speculative" concept and a fully concrete existence that corresponds to it (I,I,65). Now this judgment concerning Christianity is comprehensible only in the context of the arduous conceptual journey that its basic concept requires. But once the work is done — and it can only be done by the engagement of all the powers at one's disposal — Hegel gives assurance that one will have arrived at a criterion of religious authenticity for a religion that is neither abstract nor mysterious. "The true content of a religion is verified by the testimony of its own spirit insofar as this content is in conformity with the nature of my spirit, satisfies the needs of my spirit" (I,I,96).

Part I of Hegel's lectures on the philosophy of religion, entitled "The Concept of Religion," opens with a lengthy empirical investigation of various modes of instinctual religious certainty (*Gewissheit*) or faith, rooted in feeling and represented in primitively sensual fashion. While these are the forms in which religious experience first manifests itself, it does not ripen to maturity in them. What do they lack? In one word: thought (*Denken*). Thinking as a reflective activity is at once analytical and synthetic or syncretic: it unfolds and opens up that with which it is concerned, recognizing the internal distinctions that differentiate it from everything else even while establishing both its inherent (often latent) integrity and its interconnection with everything else. But as experienced it is closely tied to the life of the subject, and entails the rigorous activity of the negative powers of skeptical self-consciousness as they both unsettle one's inadequate present comprehension and discipline one's imaginative synthetic powers. There is no magic moment in the progress of the human mind in which thinking simply appears in serene transcendence of all other modes of cognition; on the contrary, thinking is the hard task of actively transcending these inadequate modes of representation from within and working out an acceptable reconceptualization. Man is by nature the reflective, thinking animal, and thinking is to some extent always active within him—and nowhere more appropriately than in articulating his religious and moral concerns.

The most foolish delusion of our time is the opinion that thinking is disadvantageous to religion, that religion's survival is the more secure the more it abandons thinking. This misconception stems from a thoroughly mistaken notion of the higher spiritual capacities and their interconnections. Thus in the context of ethics the good will is taken to be something that stands opposed to intelligence, and a person is credited with all the more authentic a good will the less he thinks. (I,I,155)

But for Hegel the most dismaying aspect of the religion fashionable in his own day is its subjectivism. Its content is little more than the private sentiment of the believer, which he calls his faith; it points him in the direction of an empty place, which he calls his God. There is nothing objective to ground his experiences, to bind them together into a coherent unity that he might share with his fellow men (I,I, 159–161). All the while, entrenched public authority tends to be supportive of religion in any form because of its alleged social utility, failing to realize that when religion is perceived to be subservient to mundane interests it no longer discloses the transcendental ground that inspires what is best in social and political institutions even as it underscores their natural limitations (I,I,176–180). When a people can no longer believe, its public life deteriorates and soon becomes susceptible to violence and repression (I,I,286–7). Hegel says this, realizing full well that the pages of history have been bloodied in the name of objective belief; but our capacity to pervert the meaning of an ultimate *telos* is not an argument in favor of attempting to get along without one altogether. Such a perversion generally takes the form of a defective representation; and it is the task of philosophy to remedy this by clarifying conceptually the *telos* implicit in all religious experience and representation: the meaning, the basis, and the nature of the striving that motivates the human spirit.

Now of course the content of religion is experienced and represented very differently in different times and places, and at different stages of human development. Accordingly, more than two-thirds of Hegel's text looks like a comparative history of religions, or what one might call religious anthropology. But his organizational scheme suggests more: religious history is a single, more or less coherent story, its plot being the gradual self-disclosure of something initially latent and, as it were, locked away in the very nature and constitution of humanity. Thus he investigates at some length what he calls determinate or finite religion, first in its several modes of "natural immediacy" (magic, abstract subjectivity, etc.) and then in its more advanced forms of "spiritual individuality" (beauty and sublimity, expediency and necessity). Each expresses, albeit only from its own, single perspective and somewhat out of touch with the implications of its own strivings, an essential moment of spirit and a correspondingly limited human awareness of its import. Exactly how and why each does so becomes clear only in retrospect, and most adequately at the stage of "absolute" or "manifest" religion. For only at this stage has the religious consciousness seen through the limitations and reconciled the conflicting demands of the individual representations it encompasses, thus arriving at a conceptualization as substantial as its own self-consciousness.

Now this absolute or manifest religion is indeed the Christian religion. But what Hegel proceeds to explicate as the essence of the Christian religion is considerably at variance, at least in its inner meaning, with the Christendom of the churches, schools, priests, ministers, and the market place (which he had excoriated in the early writings we have presented here). Long before the 1820's, a patient philosopher had replaced the frustrated *Volkserzieher.* At no time, to be sure, was Hegel enamored of Christendom's representation of the Incarnation as signifying that God became man in order to die for our sins—especially if this was supposed to mean that he had thereby absolved us of responsibility for them and for the spiritual challenge they pose. Civic humanist from beginning to end, Hegel always insisted that for beings who are capable of it at all, responsibility is intrinsically inalienable. Not only in "The Life of Jesus" but in his later years as well, Hegel was quite prepared to enlist the language of incarnation in the cause of a morality of freedom addressing this exact point:

> Its entry into the actual world is essential to religion, and in this passage into the world religion appears as morality with respect to the state and the totality of life. The character of a people's religion is reflected in its morality and its political constitution. These depend entirely on whether a people has grasped a merely limited notion of spirit's freedom or whether it has a true consciousness of freedom. (I,I,231)

As a corollary, from the vantage point of the speculative intellect which alone can comprehend it, the doctrine of the Atonement is more properly understood as implying that the capacity for rationality, for moral freedom and responsibility to self and others, exists at least latently in all men (II,II,160,174).

Similarly, Hegel never conceded that appeals to authority or to miracles have a valid place in the life of spirit—although he did come to make a plea for tolerance on behalf of those whose receptivity to spirit's true voice has been dulled (II,II,21–23). Attempts to buttress faith by appeal to miraculous "proofs" are self-defeating; the widespread interest in miracles stems not from piety but from curiosity, which in turn is rooted in *lack* of faith. Whereas miracles are supposed to facilitate faith, the truth is that they require it, whereas spirit itself—the only true miracle—does not (II,II,187,191).

The popular appeal of the doctrine of the soul's immortality can be explained, Hegel thinks, along similar lines: a religious consciousness fixated in sensual representations finds itself understandably incapable of actualizing the true idea of God's spiritual presence in a merely temporal here and now (II,II,178). As always, however, Hegel is less forbearing toward the populace's spiritual leaders. Their theological tracts, biblical exegeses, and Sunday sermons more often pander to or play on public sentiment than educate it. And he is still capable of stinging sarcasm when he finds the testimony of spirit being confused with the delusive concreteness of sensual immediacy:

> In the Old Testament we are told that during the exodus from Egypt red signs were placed on the doors of the Jewish houses, so that the Angel of the Lord could know which ones they were. Shouldn't the Angel have known even without these signs? (I,I,250)

Generalizing on the regressive state of religious orthodoxy in his time, Hegel seems to indulge in some special pleading for his own chosen profession:

> . . . because of the finite mode of thought that has been brought to bear on a content that is absolute, it has come to pass that the fundamental principles of Christianity have largely vanished from its official teaching. It is philosophy, not alone but in the main, that is now essentially orthodox. The propositions that have always been valid, the foundational truths of Christianity, are now preserved and maintained by philosophy. (II,II,26–7)

Not, however, by all philosophy. We have noted that as early as the 1790's Hegel was busy formulating an ideal of concrete reason as opposed to the abstractions of the formalistic understanding so widespread in the philosophy of the several schools. Subsequently, Hegel never tired of pointing out the natural affinity that such formalism has for epistemological skepticism, moral subjectivism, and ultimately a cynical view of the human condition as such. He found some tendencies in these directions even among his most outstanding and high-minded immediate predecessors. For Hegel the true meaning of divine grace (he never could accept this as something bestowed gratuitously on us by the deity) is contained in the proposition, here directed against Kant and Fichte, that "the good is not an ought-to-be, but divine power and eternal truth" (I,I,259). It was Kant who had maintained that we cannot know reality as it is in itself, but only as it appears to us; and both Kant and Fichte had described the human quest for moral and spiritual fulfillment as an endless and uncompletable task.

A medieval poet had already known better. Shortly before his death in 1831, Hegel penned these words:

> Therefore, when people assert that man cannot know the truth, they are uttering the worst form of blasphemy. They are not aware of what they are saying. Were they aware of it they would deserve that the truth should be taken away from them. The modern despair of truth being knowable is alien to all speculative philosophy as it is to all genuine religiosity. A poet who was no less religious than he was a thinker—Dante—expressed in such a pregnant fashion his belief that truth can be known, that we permit ourselves to quote his words here. He says in the Fourth Canto of the *Paradiso*, verses 124–130:

> > Io veggio ben, che giammai non si sazia
> > Nostro intelletto, se 'l *Ver* no lo illustra
> > Di fuor dal qual nessun vero si spazia
> > Posasi in esso, come fera in lustra,
> > Tosto che *giunto* l'ha; e giunger *puollo:—*
> > Se non, ciascun desio sarebbe frustra.[7]

In the Singleton translation:

> Well do I see that never can our intellect be
> wholly satisfied unless that Truth shine on it,
> beyond which no truth has range. Therein it
> rests, as a wild beast in its lair, so soon as
> it has reached it: and reach it it can, else
> every desire would be in vain.[8]

When during his last decade Hegel lectured on the Christian religion specifically, he devoted considerable attention to two doctrines,

---

7. Hegel's *Philosophy of Mind* (Part III of the *Encyclopedia of the Philosophical Sciences* [1830]), translated by William Wallace and A. V. Miller (Oxford: Clarendon Press, 1971), p. 180n.

8. Dante Alighieri, *The Divine Comedy, Paradiso*, translated by Charles S. Singleton (Princeton: Princeton University Press, 1975), p. 45. The English translation provided in the Oxford text is rather free and archaic.

For an interpretation of one aspect of Hegel's mature thought regarding these matters, see our "The Silhouette of Dante in Hegel's *Phenomenology,*" *Clio* II:4 (1982), pp. 387–413, which suggests that Hegel was consciously constructing a *Commoedia* for the modern age.

neither of which had originated in Christianity, but both of which were in it brought to the threshold of philosophical truth: Original Sin and the Incarnation. On Hegel's interpretation, the Christian view of human nature both underlies and evolves from its doctrine of Original Sin. With due allowance for its continuity with the Hebraic tradition, there appears in Christianity from the very first a dramatically heightened tension between its conception of humankind as at least potentially spiritual and thus capable of embodying a divine principle, and its bitter experience of human immediacy as inextricably mired in sin and sensuality (II,II,97). Even though divinely conceived and created, we are not by nature what we should be: Hegel considers this paradoxical vision of the human condition to be at once deeper and more realistic than the notion fashionable in his time that we are good by nature and as it were automatically, without the mediation of anything negative, and that if we should happen to fall short of perfection it is only because of some external misfortune inhibiting the satisfaction of our natural drives (II,II,102–3). This, according to Hegel, is to disregard the very tensions that make us truly human, and entails that we are not responsible for our actions, not torn between good and evil, and never guilty of anything (II,II,104).

Nonetheless, Hegel finds the representational cornerstone of Christian anthropology, i.e. its version of what happened in the Garden of Eden, to be a nest of unresolved contradictions. The first man was created morally innocent—yet succumbed to temptation and disobeyed his divine father. His sin incurred God's wrath—yet for the first time made him like unto God (the implication being that the deity must be a jealous and envious one). His fall condemned him to mortality— yet led him to the discovery of eternal life. And somehow the first man, though merely this singular individual, Adam, turned out to be representative of all men, and his sin inescapably theirs also. For Hegel all this is quite natural. The contradictions thus represented are profoundly real, only the representational understanding, forever oscillating between sense and thought, is incapable of reconciling them; speculative reason—spirit's faculty—alone can (II,II,123). Moral innocence is an animal trait, not a human one. Knowledge of good and evil (Augustine's *felix culpa*) is not per se evil; it is on the contrary what distinguishes us as humans and makes us God-like. Humanity is not a given but a task, a spiritual voyage whose signpost in effect reads: the deeper the alienation the greater the eventual reconciliation. The divine principle itself is not stasis but movement, word becoming flesh, and this movement manifests itself most fully in our species. As the philosopher reconceives it, the meaning of the Adam and Eve story centers not on who the first humans were, but on what it is to be human generically: to think, to know, and thus to partake of the eternal (II,II,127).[9]

Hegel did not find much food for thought in the Christian doctrine of the Last Judgment. But already in his early twenties he began showing a profound interest[10] in what we might call the First Judgment (*Urteil*) — the original separation (*ursprüngliche Teilung*) of the human and his divine aspect from the rest of the animal realm and indeed from his own sensual nature. This interest was sustained in his later years, during which he went so far as to conceptualize the divine process itself, i.e. the life of spirit, in terms of such an *Ur-Teilung* within a single nature.[11] Perhaps the closest thing to a last or ultimate judgment can be found in his *Logic* (or principles of ontology) when he states: "*Das Wesen muss erscheinen.*"[12] What this means is that the essence of what I produce and sustain through my reflective capacity is at some point ineluctably manifest to me in consciousness. There is no escaping this realization, this responsibility; for it is coextensive with my own consciousness in the exact measure of my intelligence. And it is thus not only the essence of a particular deed or sustained activity that is discernible; our very identity as it gradually unfolds during the course of our lives is within the purview of spirit's own powers of judgment. This is the standpoint from which Hegel's assertion that "the actual world is as it ought to be" is to be understood.[13] In response to the complaint that the ideal cannot be realized, and in fact is destroyed by cold reality, Hegel asserts that if what we mean by the ideal is a mere wish, then of course it could

9. Cf. II,II,124: "Knowledge heals the wound which it itself is." Cf. *Vorlesungen über die Geschichte der Philosophie*, II, Frankfurt am Main: Suhrkamp Verlag, 1971 (Vol. 19), p. 499.

10. Quite possibly under the influence of his close friend Hölderlin; cf. Harris, *op. cit.*, pp. 294n and 515f.

11. Cf. *Wissenschaft der Logik*, II, Suhrkamp, 1969 (Volume 6), pp. 304 and 473. Cf. the *Enzyklopädie* version of the *Logic*, #55–60, 166–67, 171–72, and 179.

12. *Logik*, II, p. 124. Hegel italicized this sentence, paragraphed it separately, and placed it at the beginning of his account of *Erscheinung*.

13. *Vorlesungen über die Philosophie der Weltgeschichte*, I, Hoffmeister edition, Hamburg: Felix Meiner, p. 77.

hardly serve as a universal principle. But the truly good—divine universal reason—which entails the principles of morality, is not a mere abstraction but the very totality of principles whereby responsible action can take place. To act in accordance with morality—whether in the form of creative endeavor, scientific inquiry, or political responsibility—is to manifest the rational universal in its particular actuality. On the other hand everything done in opposition to it, everything one produces that does not accord with it, is defective and worthless. Hence the world is as it ought to be in that the rational agent is ineluctably provided with the principles of morality as well as the means to actualize them—whereby the world can be said to embody an operative moral logic (or ontology) which neither encroaches on the freedom of the will nor denies the reality of evil, but which perfectly exposes the identity of the moral agent and unceasingly reaffirms the truth of the rational principles.

What Hegel makes of the Incarnation (and by implication of a triune Godhead) follows a similar pattern. At the level of representation and abstract understanding, this doctrine is no less contradiction-laden than is that of Original Sin. God is one and the same for all eternity—yet has a son who becomes man and dies. This he does to atone for our sins and save our souls; yet without an unprecedented spiritual effort from within on our part—indeed an *imitatio Christi*—we are not worthy of salvation. And the same Christ on earth who preaches love and brotherhood, attends so compassionately to physical need, and pays worldly power all due respect is also a revolutionary fanatic who speaks of bringing the sword, urges his followers to abandon everything earthly, even their family ties, and undermines at every opportunity all secular authority. But for Hegel, the meaning of "the Word made flesh" is not adequately comprehended unless it is conceived of necessity to embrace such antitheses. "This determination [*Bestimmung:* also destiny], that God becomes man so that finite spirit may have a consciousness of God in the finite itself, is the most difficult moment in religion" (II,II,137). Hegel knows that this must sound like blasphemy to some, but the more familiar alternative is hopelessly self-contradictory. A divinity having outside of and in opposition to itself an entrenched, independent finitude would itself be defectively infinite, that is to say finite (II,II,7). Self-differentiation or self-estrangement is of the very essence of spirit; the ensuing incommensurables (infinite/finite, spirit/flesh, etc.) are its very life, stem from its *Urteilung,* and express its infinite love (II, II,140).

"God himself is dead," so goes a Lutheran hymn. This expresses the consciousness that the human, the finite, the fragile, the weak is the divine moment itself in negative form, that it is God himself, that finitude, the negative, otherness are not external to God and that as otherness it does not prevent union with God. . . . In this is contained the highest idea of spirit. (II,II,172)

When Hegel turns to the story of Christ's life on earth, it is as though he were casting a backward glance at his concerns in 1793–1795 from the syncretic vantage point he had managed to achieve. We no longer find invidious comparisons between Socrates and Jesus. The very fact that Jesus appeared amidst such spiritual demoralization helps confirm that the spirit of Christianity is a universal one and that its morality aspires to an all-encompassing love (II,II,144f). The revolutionary extremism and the other- /and anti-worldly aspect of his teaching were necessary in order to tear the human sensibility loose from its spiritless immersion in the mundane and ephemeral (II,II,150–2). But aside from this preliminary exercise in a sort of shock therapy, the essential teaching of Christ (cf. "The Life of Jesus"), as well as that of any church worthy of bearing his name (cf. the earlier fragments), has to be couched in abstract and universal terms having a strongly rational and moral flavor. Any additional parallels between Christ and Socrates would serve only to mislead. For what is religious, and for that matter new, about Christianity is the consciousness that man and God, flesh and spirit are *absolutely* reconciled — and yet for this absolute reconciliation to be effectuated the spiritual quality of one's inner disposition is alone decisive. The recognition of the infinite worth of this *Innerlichkeit* (the term is untranslatable) brings into being a new consciousness, a new world, a new reality (II,II,154–5), by comparison with which the Socratic *Innerlichkeit,* his *daimonion,* is only a first, feeble, and as yet thoroughly "elitist" glimmering (II,II,169).

As for Christ's death, it is to be conceived as exemplary: when I manage to rise above my sense-bound will, I myself die to the merely natural and take my proper place in the life of spirit. The disgracefulness of his death served only to reinforce Christianity's revolutionary moment: the highest made lowest, the degraded exalted, strikes at the root of all conventional human values and hierarchies (II,II,159–162). We have here the Christian religion's distinctive legacy to political emancipation; before and in God all human beings are equal, free, and invested with universal rights (II,II,178f). Christ's resurrection, in turn, expresses at the representational level the consummation of the spiritual process whereby the divine Idea undergoes self-diremption and eventual reconciliation. For our kind it connotes the unqualified reception of the human into the divine (II,II,163–4). And the role of Christ's church as spiritual community is to facilitate this incarnation by educating its members to an habituated and reasoned goodness. Nothing else could as effectively silence the nagging voice of pessimism and dualism (be it in the language of Parsee theology or of Kantian philosophy), reiterating that reason and sense, externally related at best, must forever remain unalterably opposed, the one as incapable of concretion as the other is impervious to regeneration (II,II,206). Here are Hegel's concluding words:

> Philosophy is theology to this extent: It articulates that reconciliation of God with himself and nature whereby nature, otherness can itself be said to be latently divine. Finite spirits attain to this reconciliation partly on their own, but also arrive at it (or bring it about) in the course of world history. . . . This reconciliation then is the serenity of God — not something beyond all reason, but on the contrary something first known, thought through, and acknowledged as truly divine by reason. — And such a reconciliation is, on the conceptual level, the purpose of this series of lectures. (II,II,228)

The Tübingen Essay

(1793)

3   Religion is one of our greatest concerns in life. Even as children we were taught to stammer prayers to the deity, with our little hands folded for us so as to point up toward the supreme being. Our memories were laden with a mass of doctrines, incomprehensible at the time, designed for our future use and comfort in life. As we grow older, religious matters still fill up a good deal of our lives; indeed for some the whole circuit of their thoughts and aspirations is unified by religion in the way that a wheel's outer rim is linked to the hub. And we dedicate to our religion, in addition to other feast days, the first day of each week, which from earliest youth appears to us in a fairer and more festive light than all the other days. Moreover, we see in our midst a special class of people chosen exclusively for religious service; and all the more important events and undertakings in the lives of people, those on which their private happiness depends — birth, marriage, death and burial — have something religious mixed in with them.*

  But do people reflect as they become older on the nature and attributes of the being toward whom their sentiments are directed — or in particular on the relation of the world to that being? Human nature is so constituted that the practical element in sacred teaching, that in it which can motivate us to act and which becomes a source of consolation for us as well as the source of our knowledge of duty, is readily manifest to the uncorrupted human sensibility. On the other hand, the instruction (i.e. the concepts as well as everything only externally connected with [the practical]) that we receive from child-

4   hood / on, and which accordingly makes such an impression on us, is something that is, as it were, grafted onto the natural need of the human spirit. Although this relation is frequently immediate enough,

---

*[Hegel crossed out the following:] The sick and the distressed nourish themselves with the consolations of religion, which animate and sustain their hope. How many silent feelings of gratitude and devotion rise up to God — known only to him and to the praying soul.

[Editors' note: asterisks indicate Hegel's own footnotes, superscript numbers ours. The numbers in the margin indicate the pagination of the Nohl edition.]

it is, alas, all too often capricious, grounded neither in bonds indigenous to the nature of the soul nor in truths created and developed
out of the concepts . . .[1]

We should not be so enthralled by the sublime demand of reason
on mankind (the legitimacy of which we wholeheartedly acknowledge whenever our hearts happen to be filled with reason), or by
alluring descriptions (the products of pure and lovely fantasy) of wise
or innocent men, as to ever hope to find very many such people in
the real world, or to imagine that we might possess or behold this
ethereal apparition here or anywhere else. [Were we not in fact so
easily enthralled,] our sensibility would be less often clouded by a
peevish disposition, by dissatisfaction with what we in fact encounter; nor would we be so terrified when we believe ourselves obliged
to conclude that sensuality is the predominating element in all human action and striving. It is no easy matter to tell whether mere
prudence or actual morality is the will's determining ground. Granted
that the satisfaction of the instinct for happiness is the highest goal
of life, if we but know how to calculate well enough, the results will
outwardly appear the same as when the law of reason determines our
will. However scrupulously a system of morality may require us to
separate *in abstracto* pure morality from sensuality and make the latter
more subservient to the former, when we consider man's life as a whole
we must make equally full allowance for his sensuality, for his dependence on external and internal nature (i.e. both on the surroundings
in which he lives and on his sensual inclinations and blind instinct).
—But human nature is quickened, so to speak, solely by virtue of
its rational ideas. Just as a dish well prepared is permeated by salt,
which must impart its flavor to the whole without showing up in
lumps—or even as light, which cannot be exhibited as a substance,
nonetheless suffuses everything, showing its influence throughout
all nature (e.g. breaking upon objects in various ways, thus giving
them their shape, and generating wholesome air via plants, etc.)—so
likewise do the ideas of reason animate the entire fabric of our sensual
life and by their influence show forth our activity in its distinctive
light. Indeed reason as such seldom reveals itself in its essence; and

---

1. Four pages are missing at this point. The manuscript resumes with the end
of a sentence: ". . . setting in motion the [?] of human life." The paragraph continues as above ("We should not. . . ").

its effect pervades everything like fine sand, giving each and every inclination and drive a coloring of its own. /

5   By its very nature, religion is not merely a systematic investigation of God, his attributes, the relation of the world and ourselves to him, and the permanence of our souls; we could learn all this by reason alone, or be aware of it by other means. Nor is religious knowledge merely a matter of history or argumentation. Rather, religion engages the heart. It influences our feelings and the determination of our will; and this is so in part because our duties and our laws obtain powerful reinforcement by being represented to us as laws of God, and in part because our notion of the exaltedness and goodness of God fills our hearts with admiration as well as with feelings of humility and grati-tude. And so religion provides morality and the well-springs of its activity with a new and nobler impetus — it sets up a new and stronger dam against the pressure of sensual impulses. But if religious motives are to have an effect on sensuality, they too must be sensual; hence among sensual people religion itself is sensual. Of course such mo-tives, insofar as they are at all moral, lose a bit of their majesty. But they have thereby acquired such a human aspect, and have so perfectly adapted themselves to our feelings that, led by our hearts and lured on by the beauteous images of our fancy, we readily forget that cool reason disapproves of such images or indeed even forbids so much as comment on this sort of thing.

    When we go on to speak of religion as public, we still of course take it to include the concepts of God and immortality as well as everything connected with them, but specifically insofar as these con-stitute the conviction of a whole people, influencing their actions and way of thinking. Moreover, we include the means whereby these ideas are both taught to the people and made to penetrate their hearts — a means concerned not only with the immediate (e.g. I refrain from stealing because God has forbidden it), but directed more especially to ends that, while removed from the immediate, must by and large be reckoned as more important. Among these we include the uplift-ing and ennobling of the spirit of a nation so as to awaken in its soul the so often dormant sense of its true worth, and to encourage a self-image colored with the gentler hues of goodness and human-ity; for not only should it resist debasing itself or allowing itself to be degraded, but it should refuse to settle for being "merely" human.

    Now although the main doctrines of the Christian religion have

remained essentially / the same since their inception, one doctrine   6
or another has been, depending on the times and circumstances, left
altogether in the dark, while some other doctrine has been given the
limelight and, unduly emphasized at the expense of the one obscured,
stretched much too far or interpreted much too narrowly. Yet it is
the entire body of religious principles and the feelings flowing from
them—above all the degree of strength with which these are able
to influence modes of action—that is decisive in a folk religion. Upon
an oppressed spirit, one which, under the burden of its chains, has
lost its youthful vigor and begun to age, such religious ideas can have
little impact. At the beginning of maturation the youthful spirit of
a people feels its power and exults in its strength; it seizes hungrily
upon any novelty (albeit never upon anything that would put fetters
on its proud and free neck), and then typically tosses it aside in favor
of something else. By contrast, an aging spirit is characterized by its
firm attachment to tradition in every respect. It bears its fetters as
an old man endures the gout, grumbling but unable to do more. It
lets itself be pushed and shoved at its master's whim, and it is only
half conscious when it enjoys itself—not free, open, and bright with
the appealing gaiety that invites camaraderie. Moreover, its festivals
are but occasions for chatter, since old folk prefer gossip to everything
else. Here there is no boisterousness, no full-blooded enjoyment.

Exposition of the difference
between objective and subjective religion;
the importance of this exposition in view of the entire question

Objective religion is *fides quae creditur*;[2] understanding and memory
are the powers that do the work, investigating facts, thinking them
through, retaining and even believing them. Objective religion can
also possess practical knowledge, but only as a sort of frozen capital.
It is susceptible to organizational schemes: it can be systematized,
set forth in books, and expounded discursively. Subjective religion
on the other hand expresses itself only in feelings and actions. If I
say of someone that he has religion, this does not mean that he is
well schooled in it, but rather that his heart feels the active presence,

2. [the body of] faith that is [actually] being believed

the wonder, the closeness of the deity, that his heart knows or sees God in nature and in the destinies of men, that he prostrates himself before God, thanking him and glorifying him in all that he does. The actions of such an individual are not performed merely with an eye to whether they are good or prudent, but are motivated also by the thought: *This is pleasing to God*—which is often the strongest

7   motive. When something pleases him or when / he has good fortune he directs a glance at God, thanking him for it. Subjective religion is thus alive, having an efficacy that, while abiding within one's being, is actively directed outward. Subjective religion is something individual, objective religion a matter of abstraction. The former is the living book of nature, of plants, insects, birds and beasts living with and surviving off each other—each responsive to the joys of living, all of them intermingled, their various species everywhere together. The latter is the cabinet of the naturalist, full of insects he has killed, plants that are desiccated, animals stuffed or preserved in alcohol; what nature had kept totally apart is here lined up side by side; and whereas nature had joined an infinite variety of purposes in a convivial bond, here everything is ordered to but a single purpose.

The entire body of religious knowledge belonging to objective religion, then, can be the same for a large mass of people, and in principle could be so across the face of the earth. But having been woven into the fabric of subjective religion, it comprises only a small and relatively ineffectual part of it, and in fact varies within each individual. For subjective religion the chief question is whether and to what extent our sensibility is inclined to let itself be determined by religious impulses, i.e. how susceptible are we to religion sensually; then further, what makes an especially strong impression upon the heart, what kinds of feelings are most cultivated in the soul and hence most readily elicited. Some people have no feeling whatever for the more tender representations of love, so that impulses derived from the love of God simply do not affect their hearts; the organs with which they feel are rather more blunt, being roused only by the stimulus of fear (thunder, lightning, etc.). The chords of their hearts simply do not resonate to the gentle stroke of love. Other people are deaf to the voice of duty; it is quite useless to try to call their attention to the inner judge of actions which supposedly presides in man's own heart, i.e. to conscience itself. In them no such voice is ever heard; rather, self-interest is the pendulum whose swinging keeps their machine running. It is this disposition, this receptivity that determines how in each individual subjective religion is to be constituted. —We are schooled in objective religion from childhood, and our memory is laden with it all too soon, so that the as yet supple understanding, the fine and delicate plant of an open and free sensibility, is often crushed by the burden. As the roots of the plant work their way through loose soil, they absorb what they can, sucking nourishment as they go; but when diverted by a stone they seek another path. So here, too, when the burden heaped on memory cannot be dissolved, the now sturdier powers / of the soul either shake loose of it altogether or simply bypass it without drinking in any nourishment. —Yet in each person nature has planted at least the seed of finer sentiments, whose source is morality itself; she has implanted in everyone a feeling for what is moral, for ends beyond those attaching to mere sensuality. It is the task of education, of culture, to see to it that this precious seed is not choked out and is allowed to sprout into a genuine receptivity for moral ideas and feelings. And religion, precisely because it cannot be the first to take root in our sensibility, needs to find this already cultivated soil before it can flourish.

Everything depends on subjective religion; this is what has inherent and true worth. Let the theologians squabble all they like over what belongs to objective religion, over its dogmas and their precise determination: the fact is that every religion is based on a few fundamental principles which, although set forth in the different religions in varying degrees of purity, however modified or adulterated, are nonetheless the basis of all the faith and hope that religion is capable of offering us. When I speak of religion here, I am abstracting completely from all scientific (or rather metaphysical) knowledge of God, as well as from the relationship of the world and ourselves to him, etc; such knowledge, the province of discursive understanding, is theology and no longer religion. And I classify as religious only such knowledge of God and immortality as is responsive to the demands of practical reason and connected with it in a readily discernible way. (This does not preclude more detailed disclosures of special divine arrangements on man's behalf.) Further, I here discuss objective religion only insofar as it is a component of subjective religion. But I do not intend to investigate which religious teachings are of the greatest interest to the heart or can give the soul the most comfort and encouragement; nor how the doctrines of any particular religion must be constituted if they are to make a people better and happier. Rather my concern is with what needs to be done so that religion with all the force of its teaching might be blended into the fabric of human feelings, bonded with what moves us to act, and shown to be efficacious, thus enabling religion to become entirely subjective.

When it actually is so, it reveals its presence not merely by hands clasped together, knees bent, and heart humbled before the holy, but by the way it suffuses the entire scope of human inclination (without the soul being directly conscious of it) and makes its presence felt everywhere — although only mediately or, if I may so express it, negatively, in and through the cheerful enjoyment of human satisfactions. Subjective religion's role in the performance of the nobler / deeds and the exercise of the finer, philanthropic virtues is not, to be sure, a direct one; its influence is discreet, it lets the soul carry on these tasks freely and openly without inhibiting the spontaneity of its actions. Any expression of human powers, whether of courage or considerateness, cheerfulness or delight in life itself, requires freedom from an ill-natured tendency toward envy along with a conscience that is clear and not guilt-ridden; and religion helps foster both of these qualities. Furthermore, its influence is also felt insofar as innocence, when combined with it, is able to find the exact point at which delight in extravagance, high-spiritedness, and firmness of resolve would degenerate into assaults upon the rights of others.

Subjective Religion*

Inasmuch as theology (whatever its source, even if in religion) is a matter of understanding and memory, while religion is a concern of the heart stemming from a need of practical reason, it is clear that the powers of the soul activated in each of them differ considerably, and that our sensibility has to be made receptive in a different way for each. For our hope to be vindicated that the highest good — one dimension of which we are duty-bound to actualize — will become actual in its totality, our practical reason demands belief in a divinity, in immortality. —This, at any rate, is the seed from which religion

---

*[Hegel crossed out the following:]
The manner in which religion works
  a) how sensibility must be constituted if religion is to find acceptance
  b) once it has found acceptance, how does it work?

springs. But when religion is thus derived, it is in fact conscience (the inner sense of right and wrong, as well as the feeling that wrongdoing must incur punishment and welldoing merit happiness) whose elements are being analyzed and articulated in clear concepts. Now, it may well be that the idea of a mighty and invisible being first took root in the human soul on the occasion of some fearful natural phenomenon; God may first have revealed himself through weather that made everyone feel his presence more closely—if only in the gentle rustling of the evening breeze. Be that as it may, the human soul eventually experienced a moral feeling such that it found in the idea of religion something that answered to its need.

Religion is sheer superstition whenever I seek to derive from it specific grounds for action in situations where mere prudence is sufficient, or when fear of divinity makes me perform certain actions by means of which I imagine that it might be placated. / No doubt this   10
is how religion is constituted among many a sensual people. Their representation of God and how he deals with men is bound to the idea that he acts in accordance with the laws of human sensibility and acts upon their sensuality. There is little of the truly moral in this notion. However, the concept of God and my recourse to him (worship) is already more moral—hinting at consciousness of a higher order, determined by nonsensual ends (even though superstitions like the above may still be involved)—when my feeling that everything depends on God's decision leads me to beseech his support concerning the eventual outcome of an undertaking, when my belief in God's dispensing good fortune only to the just and inflicting misfortune on the unjust and presumptuous becomes at least as pervasive as belief in fate or in natural necessity, and when religion at last gives rise to principles of moral conduct.

While objective religion can take on most any color, subjective religion among good people is basically the same: what makes me a Christian in your eyes makes you a Jew in mine, Nathan says.* For religion is a matter of the heart, which often deals inconsistently with the dogmas congenial to understanding and memory. Surely the worthiest people are not always those who have done the most speculating about religion, who are given to transforming their religion into theology, and who are in the habit of replacing the fullness and warmth

*Nathan IV, 7. [Nathan the Wise (1779), an enormously influential drama by Gotthold Ephraim Lessing (1729–1781).]

of faith with cold cognitions and deft displays of verbal dexterity.

Religion in fact acquires very little through the understanding, whose operations and skeptical tendencies are more likely to chill than warm the heart. And whoever finds that other peoples' modes of representation — heathens, as they are called — contain so much absurdity that they cause him to delight in his own higher insights, his own understanding, which convinces him that he sees further than the greatest of men saw, does not comprehend the essence of religion. Someone who calls his Jehovah Jupiter or Brahma and is truly pious offers his gratitude or his sacrifice in just as childlike a manner as does the true Christian. Who is not moved by the splendid simplicity and guilelessness of someone who, when nature has bestowed its goods on him, thinks at once of his greatest benefactor and offers him the best, the most flawless, the first-born of his grain and sheep? Who does not admire Coriolanus who, at the apex of his good fortune, was mindful of Nemesis, and asked the gods / (much as Gustavus Adolphus humbled himself before God during the battle of Luetzen) not to glorify the spirit of Roman greatness but rather to make him more humble?

Such dispositions are for the heart and are meant to be enjoyed by it with simplicity of spirit and feeling, rather than be criticized by the cold understanding. Only an arrogant sectarian, fancying himself wiser than all men of other parties, could fail to appreciate the guileless last wish of Socrates to have a rooster delivered to the god of health, could remain unmoved by the beauty of his feeling in thanking the gods for death, which he regarded as a kind of convalescence, or could bring himself to make the malicious remark offered by Tertullian.[3]

A heart that does not speak louder than the understanding (unlike that of the friar in the scene from *Nathan* above), or that just keeps silent, allowing the understanding all the time it needs to rationalize

3. The full passage to which Hegel refers reads: "Idem et cum aliquid de veritate sapiebat deos negans, Aesculapio tamen gallinaceum prosecari iam in fine mandabat, credo ob honorem patris eius (Aesculapii), quia Socratem Apollo sapientissimum omnium cecinit. O Apollinem inconsideratum! Sapientiae testimonium redditit ei vero qui negabat deos esse." (Q *Septimi Tertulliani Apologeticum*, ed. C. Pascal and L. Castiglioni [Torino: Paravia and C., 1965], pp. 105–6): "Again, although he knew something of the truth and denied the gods, Socrates at the end ordered a cock to be sacrificed to Aesculapius — I think in order to honor his (Aesculapius's) father, since Apollo had declared Socrates to be the wisest of men. Careless Apollo! He had testified to the wisdom of a man who denied that the gods existed!" (translation ours)

some course of action—a heart like that isn't worth much to begin with: there is no love in it. Nowhere do we find a finer contrast between the voice of uncorrupted feeling, i.e. a pure heart, and the obstinacy of the understanding than in the Gospels. With what warmth and affection Jesus allows a woman of former ill-repute to anoint his body, accepting this spontaneous outpouring of a beautiful soul which, filled with remorse, trust, and love, refuses to be inhibited by the rabble around her. And this even as several apostles who are too cold of heart to empathize with her deepest feeling, her beautiful gift of trust, belie their pretensions to charitableness by indulging in cutting side-remarks.

What a sterile and unnatural observation it is that good old Gellert makes someplace (much like Tertullian, *Apologia*, ch. 46: *deum quilibet opifex*)[4] to the effect that a small child nowadays knows more about God than the wisest heathen. This is as if the treatise on morality I have sitting in my closet—which I can use to wrap up a stinking cheese if I see fit—were of greater value than the perhaps at times unjust heart of a Frederick the Second. For in this respect the difference between Tertullian's *opifex*, or Gellert's child who has had the theological leaven beaten into him along with the catechism, and the paper containing moral pronouncements / is on the whole not very great. A genuine consciousness acquired through experience is lacking in them to nearly the same degree. . . .[5]

12

Enlightenment: the will to actualize by means of the understanding

The understanding serves only objective religion. In clarifying fundamental principles and exhibiting them in their purity, the understanding has brought forth splendid fruit (Lessing's *Nathan*) and de-

4. The reference is apparently to the third of Christian F. Gellert's lectures on morality. Gellert (1715–1769) was best known for his poem "Der Christ." Tertullian had written: "Deum quilibet opifex Christianus et invenit et ostendit et exinde totum quod in deum quaeritur re quoque adsignat, licet Plato adfirmet factitatorum universitatis neque invenire facile et inventum enarrari in omnes difficile." "Any Christian workman discovers God and demonstrates his presence, attributing to him everything one looks for in God. And yet Plato can assert that the maker of the universe is not easy to find, and is hard to describe to everyone even when he is found." (translation ours)

5. Here in all likelihood one sheet (roughly eight pages) are missing.

serves the eulogies with which it is forever being extolled. But such principles are never made practical by means of the understanding alone.

The understanding is a courtier who is ruled complaisantly by the moods of his master. It knows how to hunt up rationalizations for every passion, every venture; and it is first and foremost a servant of self-love, which is always very clever at putting blunders committed or about to be committed in a favorable light. Self-love likes to sing its own praises for this, i.e. for having found such a good excuse for itself.

Having my understanding enlightened does make me smarter, but not better. If I reduce virtue itself to shrewdness, and calculate that no one can become happy without it, such a calculation is much too sophisticated and cold to be effective in the moment of action, indeed to have any influence on my life at all.

Were one to adopt the very best of moral codes, inform oneself most exactly both about its universal principles and its derivative duties and virtues, and keep in mind this mountain of rules and exceptions at the moment of action, the result would be a mode of conduct so involuted that one would be eternally hesitant and at odds with oneself. Not even the authors of moral codes go so far as to expect that somebody would actually commit their books to memory or, upon the slightest impulse to action, consult them before doing anything in order to ensure that this is all quite ethical and hence permissible. And yet this is in fact what one demands of a person when one insists on a moral code. No printed code or manner of enlightening the understanding could ever prevent evil impulses from taking root or even flourishing. In view of this, Campe's *Theophron*[6] is designed to have only a negative effect — a person ought to act on his own, work things out / for himself, make his own decisions, not let anybody else do this for him — although in his hands this ap-

13

6. J. H. Campe: *Theophron oder der erfahrene Ratgeber für die unerfahrene Jugend* (Hamburg, 1783) [*Theophron or the Experienced Counsellor for Inexperienced Youth*]. This work came into Hegel's possession in 1785, while he was at the Gymnasium. The Suhrkamp editors' interpretation of this passage strikes us as implausible. It requires three interpolations: "diese negative Wirkung [erstrebt] Campes *Theophron* — [nicht:] der Mensch soll selbst handeln. . . , [sondern er] ist da nichts wieter als blosse Maschine." This version would read: "this negative effect is what Campe's *Theophron* [aims at] — [not:] the individual should . . . him [but rather he] is there nothing more than a mere machine."

proach turns out to be nothing more than a mechanical contrivance.

When one speaks of enlightening a people, this presupposes that errors and vulgar prejudices associated with religion are rampant. And by and large religions do consist of such things, based as they are on sensuousness—on the blind expectation that a certain effect will be brought about by an alleged cause that has nothing to do with it. Among a people full of prejudices the concept of cause seems largely based on the notion of mere succession, as evidenced by its not infrequent tendency, when speaking of causes, to leave out and indeed fail to observe the intermediate members of a series of effects. Hence sensuousness and fantasy are and remain the sources of prejudice. And even valid propositions that have stood up to investigation by the understanding are still prejudices when people simply adopt and give credence to them without having any rational grounds for them.

Prejudices, therefore, can be of two kinds:

a) notions that are actually erroneous,

b) notions that, while in actuality true, are not apprehended as truths ought to be (i.e. by means of reason), being acknowledged only on the basis of trust or faith, and thus doing little credit to the person who accepts them. To enlighten a people, to rid it of its intellectual prejudices (practical prejudices, i.e. those that affect the determining process of the will, have entirely different sources and consequences and are thus of no concern here) involves improving its understanding in certain respects so that it may free itself of the thrall of error and attain the certainty of actual truths on rational grounds. Yet to begin with, who is the mortal willing to decide what truth is? Still, we can here assume—as we must when we speak of human knowledge in concreto and (from a political perspective) in view of the fact that human societies do exist—that surely there are some universally valid principles which are not only evident to common sense but form the basis of any religion deserving of the name, however deformed it may be.

α) Certainly there are only a few such principles; and they are all quite general and abstract. Thus when set forth in their purity as reason demands, they "contradict" ordinary experience as well as everything that seems so apparent to the senses. These they could never influence anyhow, since / they are fit only for an order of things antithetic to sense. Little wonder, then, that they do not readily qualify for whole-hearted acceptance on the part of the people. And even

14

if they are preserved in memory, they still constitute no part of man's system of spiritual desires.

β) Now a religion that is supposed to be generally accessible cannot consist just of some universal truths embraced lovingly and whole-heartedly only by the handful of outstanding individuals who redis-covered them for their era. Hence there are always added ingredients which must be taken merely on faith; and the purer tenets must be coarsened and given a more sensual exterior if they are to be under-stood and made accessible to a sensual disposition. Moreover, cus-toms must be introduced that require, if one is to be aware of their necessity and utility, either trusting belief or habituation from child-hood on. Thus it is evident that a folk religion, if as its very concept implies its teaching is to be efficacious in active life, cannot possibly be constructed out of sheer reason. Positive religion necessarily rests on faith in the tradition by which it is handed down to us. Our com-mitment to religious customs stems likewise from their binding force, i.e. from our belief that God demands them of us as being appropri-ate and obligatory. But when they are taken merely by themselves and regarded rationally, all that can be claimed for them is that they serve to edify, to awaken pious sentiments; and their suitability for this purpose is always open to critical inspection. Yet as soon as I have persuaded myself that such customs and forms of worship do no real honor to God—that right conduct is the form of service most pleasing to him—they have, despite their edifying effect, thereby al-ready lost a good deal of their potential impact on me.

Since religion is inherently a matter of the heart, one might well ask how much ratiocination it can tolerate without ceasing to be reli-gion. If we do a lot of reflecting on the formation of our sentiments—on the customs in which we are made to participate and which are supposed to awaken pious feelings, on their historical origin, on their utility, and so forth—they surely lose some of the aura of sanctity with which we had always been accustomed to regard them. No less do the dogmas of theology lose some of their dignity when we look at them in the light of ecclesiastical history. Yet how little lasting effect such cool reflections have can be seen when we find ourselves in straitened circumstances, when a troubled heart seeks a sturdier 15 staff, when in desperation / we reach out—deaf to the sophistries of the understanding—for anything that once gave comfort, clutching at it all the more tightly and fearfully now lest it slip away again.

Wisdom is something quite different from enlightenment, from ratiocination. But wisdom is not science. Wisdom is the soul's elevation, through experience deepened by reflection, over its dependence on opinion and the impressions of sense. And if it is to be practical and not merely a complacent and boastful intellectualism, wisdom must be attended by the steady warmth of a gentle flame. It does little rationalizing; and it does not proceed *methodo mathematica* from concepts and, by way of a series of inferences in the mode of Barbara and Barocco, arrive at what it takes to be truth. Nor does it purchase its conviction at the common marketplace, where knowledge is handed out to anybody who pays the right price; indeed it wouldn't know what denomination to put on the counter for such a deal. —And when it speaks, it does so only from the depths of its heart.

Now the cultivation of the understanding and its application to matters that elicit our interest may very well be promoted by enlightenment—along with a firm grasp of our obligations and a clear head in practical matters. But none of these are such that they could endow mankind with morality. They are infinitely inferior in worth to goodness and purity of heart, with which they are not really commensurable in the first place.

A happy disposition is a major part of the character of a well-constituted youth. But now suppose that circumstances compel this youth to become increasingly self-absorbed, and he resolves to cultivate himself into a virtuous person. Lacking the experience to realize that books cannot make him one, he may perhaps pick up Campe's *Theophron* in order to make its lessons in wisdom and prudence the guiding principles of his life. Each morning and evening he reads an excerpt, and all day he thinks about it. What will be the result? True self-perfection, perhaps? Knowledge of human nature? Practical good sense? All this requires years of experience and practice—yet meditation on Campe and the Campian rule will cure him in a week! Gloomily and apprehensively he enters into a society where only those are welcome who know how to be amusing. Timidly he indulges in this or that pleasure which is a real treat only for him who partakes of it cheerfully. Overcome by feelings of inferiority, he defers to everyone. The company of women gives him no joy, / for he fears   16 that even the slightest contact with some girl might cause a raging fire to course through his veins. His appearance is awkward, his demeanor rigid. But he won't be able to stand this for long; soon he will reject his peevish mentor's outlook on life, and feel all the better for it.

If enlightenment is to accomplish what its eulogists claim for it, if it is to earn its accolades, it must become true wisdom. Short of this it tends to remain a kind of snobbish sophistry that fancies itself superior to its many weaker brethren. Such arrogance is typical of adolescents, and indeed of their elders; having got a couple of insights out of books, they begin scoffing at beliefs they had up to now, like everyone else, unquestioningly accepted. In this process vanity of course plays a major role. So whenever someone has a great deal to say about the incomprehensible stupidity of the masses, seeks to show at great length that some popular prejudice is the most unbelievable folly, and is given to bandying about terms like 'enlightenment', 'the knowledge of human nature,' 'the history of mankind', 'happiness' and 'perfection', we know we are in the presence of one of enlightenment's babbling quacks peddling shopworn panaceas. These types stuff each other with empty words, oblivious to the sacred and delicate web of human feeling. Everyone is likely to hear examples of such idle chatter; no doubt some have experienced it firsthand already, for in our wordy age this form of culture is quite prevalent. Even if life itself gives one or another of us a better understanding of what had previously been stashed away in our soul as unused capital, we still have to deal with a bellyfull of book learning which, undigested, keeps the stomach hard at work, precluding healthier nourishment and preventing the flow of nutrients to the rest of the body. Our corpulence may give the appearance of health, but in every joint our free movement is inhibited by dried-out phlegm.

Part of the business of enlightened understanding is to refine objective religion. But when it comes to the improvement of mankind (the cultivation of strong and great dispositions, of noble feelings, and of a decisive sense of independence), the powers of the understanding are of little moment; and the product, objective religion, doesn't carry much weight either. Human understanding is nonetheless rather flattered when it contemplates its work: a grand and lofty 17 edifice of knowledge divine, / moral, and natural. And true enough, it has provided out of its own resources the building materials for this edifice which it is making ever more elaborate. But as this building, which engages the efforts of humanity as a whole, becomes gradually more extensive and complex, it becomes less and less the property of any one individual. Anybody who simply copies this universal structure or appropriates it piecemeal — anybody who does not build within (and indeed from inside) himself a little residence of his own, roofed and framed so that he feels at home in it, with every stone if not hewn then at least laid by his own hands — anybody who neglects to do this becomes a person who can only rigidly adhere to the letter, who has never really lived.

And were the individual to have this great house rebuilt for him as a palace, and inhabit it as Louis xiv did Versailles, he would have only the barest acquaintance with its many chambers and would actually occupy a mere cubicle. By contrast, a family man is far more familiar with the details of his ancestral home, and can give an account of every bolt and every little cabinet, telling what they are used for now as well as their history (Lessing's *Nathan:* "For the most part I can still tell how, where, and why I learned it.").[7] —This little house, which he can indeed call his own, requires the help of religion to build; but how much can religion help in all this?

The difference between a pure religion of reason, which worships God in spirit and in truth, affirming that he is served through virtue alone, and an idolatrous faith, which imagines it can curry God's favor by some means other than a will that is in itself good, is so great that in comparison the latter is utterly worthless. In fact the two are completely different in kind. It is nonetheless of the utmost importance for us to discourage any fetishistic mode of belief, to make it more and more like a rational religion. Yet a universal church of the spirit remains a mere ideal of reason; and it is hardly possible to establish a public religion that would really do everything it could to rid itself of fetishistic belief. So the question naturally arises: How would a folk religion have to be constituted so that a) negatively, the opportunity for people to become fixated on the letter and the conventions of religion would be minimized, and b) positively, the people would be guided toward a religion of reason and become receptive to it?

Whenever moral philosophy posits the idea of saintliness as consisting of moral conduct at its highest, of moral exertion to the fullest, the objection will be raised that such an idea is beyond / human attainment (which the moral philosophers themselves concede) be-

against Kant

18

---

7. *Nathan,* V, 6.

cause man needs motives other than pure respect for the moral law, motives more closely bound up with his sensuality. Such an objection does not prove that man ought not to strive, for all eternity if need be, to approximate to this idea, but merely that, given our crudeness and our powerful propensity toward the sensual, one ought to be content to elicit from most people a mere legality that does not demand the kind of purely moral motives (cf. Matt. 19:16) for which they feel little or no affinity. Nor does such an objection deny that much has already been gained if crude sensuality is at least in some way refined and *some* interest in higher things is aroused—if propensities are awakened other than sheer animal drives, ones more amenable to the influence of reason and approximating to morality a little more closely. For in this way it is at least possible that, whenever the clamor of the senses dies down a little, moral dispositions might begin to make their presence known. In fact it is generally conceded that cultivation of *any* kind would already be a gain. Hence what this objection really comes down to is that it is altogether unlikely that humankind, or even a single individual, will ever in this world be able to dispense entirely with nonmoral promptings.

Now we do in fact have a number of feelings, woven into our very nature, which do not arise out of respect for the law and hence are not moral, which are inconstant and unstable and do not deserve respect because of any inherent worth, but which are nevertheless to be cherished because they serve to inhibit evil dispositions and even help bring out the best in us. All the benign inclinations (sympathy, benevolence, friendliness, etc.) are of this sort. But this empirical aspect of our character, confined as it is to the arena of the inclinations, does contain a moral sentiment bent on weaving its delicate thread throughout the entire fabric. Indeed the fundamental principle of our empirical character is love, which is somewhat analogous to reason in that it finds itself in other people. Forgetting about itself, love is able to step outside of a given individual's existence and live, feel, and act no less fully in others—just as reason, the principle of universally valid laws, recognizes its own self in the shared citizenship each rational being has in an intelligible world. The empirical character of human beings is still of course affected by desire and aversion; but love, even though as a principle of action it is subrational,[8] is not

8. Hegel has here "ein pathologisches Prinzip des Handelns." He is following

self-serving. It does not do the right thing merely because it has cal-
culated that the satisfactions resulting from its course of action are
purer and longer lasting than those resulting from sensuality or the
gratification of some passion. This principle, then, is not refined self-
love, in which the ego is in the end always the highest goal. /

Empiricism is of course absolutely useless in the establishment of 19
foundational principles. But when it comes to having an effect on
people, we must take them as they are, seeking out every decent drive
and sentiment through which, albeit without directly enhancing their
freedom, their nature can be ennobled. In a folk religion in particular
it is of the utmost importance that the imagination and the heart
not be left unsatisfied: the imagination must be filled with large and
pure images, and the heart roused to feelings of benevolence. Setting
these on a sound course is all the more crucial in the context of religion, whose object is so great and sublime; for both the heart and
the imagination all too easily strike out on paths of their own or
let themselves be led astray. The heart is seduced by false notions and
by its own indolence; it becomes attached to externals, or finds sus-
tenance in feelings of false modesty, thinking that with these it serves
God. And the imagination, taking to be cause and effect what is
merely accidental, comes to expect the most extraordinary and unnatural results. Man is such a many-sided creature that anything can
be made of him; the intricately woven fabric of his feelings has so
many strands that there is nothing that cannot be attached to it at
some point. This is why he has been capable of the silliest superstitions, and of the greatest ecclesiastical[9] and political slavery. Folk religion's primary task is to weave these fine strands into a noble union
suitable to his nature.

The main difference between folk religion and private religion is
one of aim. Through the mighty influence it exerts on the imagination and the heart, folk religion imbues the soul with power and enthusiasm, with a spirit indispensable for the noble exercise of virtue.
On the other hand, the training of individuals in keeping with their
character, counsel in situations where duties conflict, special inducements to virtue, comfort and care in the face of personal suffering

---

a philosophical convention, owing much to Kant, according to which 'pathological'
is contrasted with 'rational' and has no connotation of disease.

9. H. S. Harris is surely right in translating *hierarchischen* this way.

and misfortune—all such things must be left to private religion. That this is not the concern of a public folk religion is evident from the following considerations:

a) Situations that involve a conflict of duties are so complex that I can satisfy my conscience only by falling back on the counsel of upright and experienced men or by recourse to the conviction that [come what may] duty and virtue constitute the highest principle of conduct—assuming of course that this conviction has been in some way established by public religion and so become available to me as a maxim of action. But public instruction, like the moral training mentioned above, is too tedious; and not even this conviction is in the least capable of making us / amenable in the moment of action to hair-splitting casuistical rules. If it were, the result would be a perpetual scrupulosity quite contrary to the resoluteness and strength requisite for virtuous action.

b) If virtue is not the product of indoctrination and empty rhetoric but is rather a plant which, albeit with proper tending, grows out of one's own driving force and power, then the various arts invented allegedly to produce virtue as though in a hothouse (where it would be incapable of failure) actually do more damage to people than just letting them grow wild. By its very nature public religious instruction involves not only an attempt to enlighten the understanding concerning the idea of God and our relation to him, but also an effort to make our obligations to God the ground of all other duties, whereby the latter become at once more urgent and more binding. But there is something strained and farfetched about this derivation. It involves a relationship whose connection only the understanding comprehends, one that tends to be rather forced and is not at all evident, at least to common sense. Ordinarily, the more inducements we are offered for doing our duty, the cooler we become toward it.

c) The only true comfort in suffering (for pain [*Schmerzen*][10] there is no comfort; strength of soul is all that can be pitted against it) is trust in divine providence. Everything else is idle talk which the heart does not heed.

10. Cf. Harris, p. 498, note 2, for a variant reading (Schmerzen: sorrows) based on certain passages in Hegel's subsequent essays. But given the fragmentary character of Hegel's remark here, the naturalness of the distinction as we have it, and (as Harris notes) its isolated occurrence in this collection of texts, we find neither interpretation conclusive.

How is a folk religion to be constituted? (Here folk religion is understood in an objective sense.)

a) With respect to objective religion.

b) With respect to ceremonies.

A. I. Its teachings must be founded on universal reason.

II. Imagination, the heart, and the senses must not go away empty-handed in the process.

III. It must be so constituted that all of life's needs, including public and official transactions, are bound up with it.

B. What must it avoid?

Fetishistic beliefs, including one that is especially common in our prolix age, namely the belief that the demands of reason are satisfied by means of / tirades against enlightenment and the like. As a result, 21 people are endlessly at loggerheads over points of dogma without doing anything constructive either for themselves or for anyone else.

I

The doctrines [of a folk religion], even if resting on the authority of some divine revelation, must of necessity be constituted so that they are actually authorized by the universal reason of mankind, whereby one is no sooner made aware of them than he perceives and recognizes their binding force. For even if such doctrines either claim to furnish special means of obtaining God's favor or promise all sorts of privileged insights and detailed information concerning otherwise inaccessible matters, the disclosures they provide are intended to serve one's rational intellect, not just one's fantasy. Moreover, since doctrines such as these sooner or later come under fire from thinking men and end up as objects of controversy, our practical interest in them invariably gets misdirected as the endless bickering of various factions issues in rigid symbols expressive of little but their own intolerance. And since these doctrines remain unnatural in their link to the true needs and demands of rationality, they lend themselves to abuses, especially as they become engrained and hardened through habit. Surely they could never of themselves gain sufficient weight in human feeling to be a pure and genuine force in direct alignment with morality.

But the doctrines must also be simple; and indeed they are simple, if only they be truths of reason, because as such they require neither the machinery of erudition nor a display of laborious demonstrations. By virtue of such simplicity, they would exert all the more power and impact on our sensibility, on the determination of our will to act; thus concentrated, they would have a far greater influence and play a much bigger part in cultivating a people's spirit than is the case when commandments are piled up and ordered artificially so as always to be in need of many exceptions.

At the same time, these universal doctrines must be designed for humans, i.e. must be in keeping with the level of morality and spiritual cultivation attainable by a given people—which is no easy task to determine. Some of the noblest—and for mankind most interesting—ideas are scarcely suited for adoption as universal maxims. They appear to be appropriate only for a handful of ripened individuals who, having endured many trials, have already succeeded in attaining wisdom. In such individuals they have become sure beliefs, and in situations / where such beliefs are truly supportive they have become matters of unshakable conviction. Thus, for instance, the belief in a wise and benevolent providence: when it is alive and of the right sort, it goes hand in hand with the complete acceptance of God's will.

Now this tenet and everything connected with it is also undeniably the main doctrine of the whole Christian community, whose teachings in general reduce to the all-transcending love of God toward which everything moves. Day in and day out God is represented to us as being ever present and close by, as bringing about everything that goes on around us. And this is not just represented as being somehow necessarily linked with our morality and everything we hold sacred, it is even given out as a matter of complete certainty on the basis of the abundant assurances God provides us and through all the deeds he performs to convince us of it incontrovertibly. And yet as experience teaches, a mere thunderclap or a cold night can cause the masses to become very faint-hearted in their trust in divine providence and in their patient submission to God's will, it evidently being only within the capability of the wise man to quell impatience and anger over frustrated hopes, and to overcome despair over misfortunes. Such abrupt abandonment of trust in God, this sudden changeover to dissatisfaction with him, is facilitated not only by accustoming the Christian populace from childhood on to pray incessantly, but even more by forever seeking to persuade it of the most urgent necessity for doing so through promises that such prayers will surely to some degree be answered.

Moreover, suffering mankind has been furnished with such a motley assortment of reasons for proffering solace in misfortunes that in the end one might well come to regret not having a father or mother to lose once a week, or not being struck blind. With incredible acuity, this way of thinking has taken to pursuing and pondering over the widest range of physical and moral effects. And since these were alleged to be the designs of Providence, it was supposed that one had herewith attained keener insight into its plans for humankind, both in the broad perspective and in detail. — But no sooner do we lose patience with this, unwilling to merely lay our finger across our lips and lapse into awe-stricken silence, than we tend to find ourselves prey to an arrogant inquisitiveness that presumes to nothing short of mastery of the ways of Providence — a propensity reinforced (though not among the common people) by the many idealistic notions currently in vogue. All of which contributes little indeed to the furthering of contentment / with life in general and acquiescence in   23 God's will.

It might be interesting to compare all this with what the Greeks believed. On the one hand, their faith — that the gods favor those who are good, and leave evildoers to the tender mercies of a frightful Nemesis — was based on a profoundly moral demand of reason and lovingly animated by the warm breath of their feelings, rather than on the cold conviction, deduced from single instances, that everything turns out for the best (a conviction that can never come truly alive). On the other hand, among them misfortune was misfortune, pain was pain. What had happened could not be altered. There was no point in brooding over whatever such things might mean, since their *moira*, their *anangkaia tyche*,[11] was blind. But then they submitted to this necessity willingly and with all possible resignation. And at least this much can be said in their favor: one endures more easily what one has been accustomed from childhood on to regard as necessary, and that the pain and suffering to which misfortune naturally gives birth did not occasion in them the much more burdensome and

11. The Greek phrase *anangkaia tyche* designates necessity, fate, or fortune; *moira* refers to one's destiny or lot in life.

unbearable anger, the despondency and discontent we feel. This faith, since it embraced not only respect for the course of natural necessity but also the conviction that men are governed by the gods in accordance with moral laws, seems humanly in keeping with the exaltedness of the divine and the frailty of man in his limited perspective and dependence on nature.

Doctrines that are simple and founded upon universal reason are compatible with every stage of popular education. And the latter comes gradually to modify the former in accordance with its own transformations, albeit more with respect to its external effects, i.e. those having to do with what the sensuous imagination depicts.

In keeping with how they are constituted, these doctrines, if they are founded on universal human reason, can have no other purpose than to influence the spirit of a people in but a general way — and to do so partly in and of themselves and partly through the closely connected magic of powerfully impressive ceremonies. They have no business interfering in the execution of civil justice or usurping the role of one's private conscience. Nor, since the way in which they are formulated is simple as well, will they easily give rise to squabbles over their meaning. And, since they demand and stipulate very little that is positive (reason's legislation being in any event merely formal), the lust for power on the part of the priests of such a religion remains circumscribed.

II

Any religion purporting to be a folk religion must be so constituted that it engages the heart and imagination. Even the purest / religion of reason must become incarnate in the souls of individuals, and all the more so in the people as a whole. In order that our fantasy be given a proper outlet, one orienting it onto a path it can decorate with its beautiful flowers without drifting off into romantic extravagances, it would be best to tie myths to the religion itself from the very outset. Now the doctrines of the Christian religion are for the most part tied to history and represented historically. The stage, even if other than mere humans acted on it, is set here in this mundane realm. Thus our imagination is provided with a readily discernible goal. To be sure, our imagination is still given some room to rove:

if colored with black bile it can paint a frightful world for itself, or —
since the spirit of our religion has banished all the beautiful colora-
tions of sense as well as everything that has charm, even while we
have become far too much men of words and reason to take much
delight in beautiful images — it may well lapse into childishness.

With regard to ceremonies, on the one hand no folk religion is
conceivable without them; on the other, nothing is harder to prevent
than their being taken by the populace at large for the essence of religion
itself. Now religion consists of three things: a) concepts, b) essential
customs, and c) ceremonies. Thus if we regard baptism and the eucharist as rites involving certain extraordinary benefits and indulgences
which we as Christians are duty-bound to perform so as to become
more perfect, more moral, then they belong to the second class. But
if we look upon them as mere means intended and able only to arouse
pious sentiments, then they belong to the third class. — Sacrifices belong here too; but they cannot properly be called ceremonies, for they
are essential to the religion with which they are connected. They are
part of its structure, whereas ceremonies are mere embellishments,
the formal aspect of this structure.

Sacrifices themselves can be looked at from two perspectives:

a) In part they were brought to the altars of the gods as propitiation, as atonement, as an attempt either to commute a much-feared
physical or moral punishment into a fine or to ingratiate oneself into
the lost favor of the supreme lord, the dispenser of rewards and punishments. Such practices are of course deemed unworthy and rightly
censured on grounds of their irrationality and their adulteration of
the whole concept of morality. But we have to keep in mind that
an idea of sacrifice as crass as this has never really gained ascendancy
anywhere (except perhaps / in the Christian church),* and we have
to appreciate the value of the feelings activated in the process, even
if they were not pure: a solemn awe of the holy being, a contrite
heart humbly prostrated before him, and the deep trust that drove
a troubled soul crying out for peace to this anchor. Think of a pilgrim burdened by the weight of his sins. He has left behind the comforts of home, his wife and children, his native soil, to wander through

25

*Outside the Christian church a sacrifice was at most a drop of balm for the
soul of the offender; his conscience (for surely there is no instance of such a degree
of moral corruption among a [more primitive] people) was not so easily pacified.

the world barefoot and clad in a hair-shirt. He hunts for impassable tracts to torment his feet. He sprinkles the holy places with his tears. Seeking repose for his ravaged spirit, he finds relief in every tear shed, in every mortification. He is urged on by the thought "Here Christ walked, here he was crucified for me," a thought from which he gains renewed strength, renewed self-confidence. — But is it really for us, incapable of such a state of mind merely because of other notions prevalent in our time, to react to such a pilgrim and such simplicity of heart with the Pharisaic sentiment "Well, I am more sensible than people like that"? Is it for us to heap ridicule upon his pious sentiments? Then again, expiatory pilgrimages like this do form a subspecies of precisely the sort of sacrifice I was speaking of above, being offered up in the very same spirit as those penances.

b) But there is another, milder spirit of sacrifice, one germinating in a gentler latitude, that was probably the more original and universal. It was based on gratitude and benevolence. Filled with the sense of a being higher than man, and aware of its indebtedness to him for everything, it was confident that he would not scorn what was offered him in all innocence. It was disposed to implore his help at the outset of every undertaking, and to sense his presence in every joyous experience, every good fortune attained. Thinking of Nemesis before partaking of any pleasure, it offered to its god the first fruits, the flower of every possession, inviting him into its home confident that he would abide there willingly. The frame of mind that offered such a sacrifice was far removed from any notion of having hereby atoned for its sins or expiated some portion of their justly deserved punishment. Nor did its conscience persuade it that in this manner Nemesis might be appeased and induced to give up not only / her claims on it but her laws governing the restoration of moral equilibrium as well.

Essential practices like these need not be bound more closely to religion than to the spirit of the people; it is preferable that they actually spring from the latter. Otherwise their exercise is without life, cold and powerless, and the attendant feelings artificial and forced. On the other hand it may be that these are practices that are not essential to folk religion anyway, although they may be to private religion. Thus for instance we have the eucharist as it exists in its present form throughout Christendom, although originally it was intended as a meal for communal enjoyment.

The indispensable characteristics of ceremonies designed for a folk religion are:

a)[12] First and foremost, that they contain little or no inducement to fetishistic worship—that they not consist of a mere mechanical operation devoid of spirit. Their sole aim must be to intensify devotion and pious sentiments. Perhaps the only pure means for eliciting such an effect, the one least susceptible to misuse, is sacred music and the song of an entire people—perhaps also folk festivals, in which religion is inevitably involved.

III

As soon as any sort of wall is put between doctrine and life—as soon as they become in any way separated or lose touch with each other—we begin suspecting that there is something wrong with the very form of this religion. Perhaps it is too preoccupied with empty verbiage. Perhaps excessive and hypocritical demands are being made on the people, demands repugnant to their natural needs, to the impulses of a well-ordered sensibility (*tes sophrosynes*).[13] Or possibly both at once. If a religion makes people feel shame over their moments of joy and merriment, if someone has to slink into the temple because he has made a spectacle of himself at a public festival, then its outer form is too forbidding for it to expect anyone to give up life's pleasures in favor of its demands.

A folk religion must be a friend to all life's feelings; it should never intrude, but should seek to be a welcome guest everywhere. And if it is to have real effect on a people, it must also be their companion—supportive of their undertakings and the more serious concerns of their lives as well as of their festivals and times of fun. It must not appear obtrusive, must not become a nagging schoolmarm, but rather initiate and encourage. The folk festivals of the / Greeks were all religious festivals, and were held either in honor of a god or of a man deified because of his exemplary service to his country. They consecrated everything, even their bacchantic excesses, to some deity; and

12. There is no *h*

13. The Greek *tes sophrosynes* can very well mean, as Hegel has it, "of a well-ordered sensibility," i.e. one that is imbued with temperance.

the dramas they staged in the public theater had a religious origin which they never disavowed, even as they became more cultivated. Thus, for instance, Agathon did not forget the gods when he carried off a prize for his tragedy; the very next day he arranged a feast for them (*Sympos.*, p. 168).[14]

A folk religion—engendering and nurturing, as it does, great and noble sentiments—goes hand in hand with freedom. But our religion would train people to be citizens of heaven, gazing ever upward, making our most human feelings seem alien. Indeed at the greatest of our public feasts we proceed to the enjoyment of the holy eucharist dressed in the colors of mourning and with eyes downcast; even here, at what is supposed to be a celebration of human brotherhood, we fear we might contract venereal disease from the brother who drank out of the communal chalice before. And lest any of us remain attentive to the ceremony, filled with a sense of the sacred, we are nudged to fetch a donation from our pocket and plop it on a tray. How different were the Greeks! They approached the altars of their friendly gods clad in the colors of joy, their faces, open invitations to friendship and love, beaming with good cheer.

The spirit of a nation is reflected in its history, its religion, and the degree of its political freedom; and these cannot be taken in isolation when considering either their individual character or their influence on each other. They are bound together as one, like three companions none of whom can do anything without the others even as each benefits from all. The improvement of individual morality is a matter involving one's private religion, one's parents, one's personal efforts, and one's individual situation. The cultivation of the spirit of the people as a whole requires in addition the respective contributions of folk religion and political institutions.* /

14. Hegel's reference is to the Stephanus edition of the *Symposium*. Cf. Harris, p. 505n.

*The father of this spirit is Chronos (Time), on whom he remains to some extent dependent all his life (temporal circumstances). His mother is the politeia, the constitution. His midwife, his wet-nurse, is religion, which enlists the aid of the fine arts, especially music, in order to give form to the movement of his spirit and body. His is an ethereal being which, though drawn down to earth and held there by a slender thread, resists with the help of a magic spell all attempts to break it, for it is completely entwined in his essence. This thread, whose coarse grain is animal desire, is woven together out of myriad natural fibers. Since with each new fiber he is bound more tightly to nature, he feels so little weighed down that he experi-

Ah, to the soul that retains a feeling for human splendor, for great-   28
ness in great things, there radiates from distant bygone days an un-
forgettable image. It is the picture of the spirit of nations, son of
fortune and freedom, pupil of a fine imagination. He too was tied
to mother earth by the brazen fetters of basic need. But by means
of his sensibility and imagination he cultivated, refined, and beauti-
fied them to such an extent that, garlanded with roses given by the
Graces, he was able in the midst of these chains to take delight in
them as his own handiwork, as part of his own self. His servants
were joy, gaiety, and poise, and his soul was suffused with the consciousness of its power and freedom. But his more intimate playmates
were friendship and love — not the wood faun but sensitive, soulful
Amor, adorned with all the allurements of the heart and of sweet
dreams.

Thanks to his father, himself a favorite of Fortune and a son of
Force, he had ample trust in his own destiny and took pride in his
deeds. His warm-hearted mother, never harsh or reproachful, left her
son to nature's nurturing; good mother that she was, she refused to
cramp his delicate limbs in tight swaddling. She would rather play
along with the moods and inspirations of her darling than think to
curb them; in harmony with these, his nurse [i.e. religion] reared this
child without fear of the rod or ghosts in the dark, without the bit-
tersweet honey bread of mysticism or the fetters of words which would
keep him perpetually immature. Instead she had him drink the clear
and healthful milk of pure sensations. With the flowers of her fine
and free imagination she adorned the impenetrable veil that removes
the deity from our gaze, conjuring up behind it a realm inhabited
by living images onto which he projected the great ideas his heart
brings forth in all the fullness of its noble and beautiful sentiments.
Just as the nanny in ancient Greece was a friend of the family and
remained a friend of her charge the rest of her life, so his nurse [again,
religion] remains his friend even while he, unspoiled as he is, freely

---

ences on the contrary an expansion of his pleasures, a broadening of his life, as he
willingly senses these fibers spontaneously enlarge and multiply. Gradually all the
finer, more delicate feelings ripen within him, feelings which through social inter-
action bring him a thousand modulations of delight. [Ed. note: This passage actually occurs in the main text and not as a footnote. But as Professor Harris rightly
notes, Hegel cancelled this passage "some time after he had written it."]

expresses his gratitude and returns her love. A good companion, she shares in his pleasures and takes part in his games; and he in turn 29 never finds her a bother. / Yet she always maintains her dignity; and his conscience rebels whenever he slights it. Her dominion holds sway forever, for it is based on the love, the gratitude, the noblest feelings of her ward. She has coaxed their refinement along, she has obeyed his imagination's every whim—yet she has taught him to respect iron necessity, she has taught him to conform to this unalterable destiny without murmur.

We know this spirit only by hearsay. We have only a few traces on a handful of surviving reproductions that enable us to contemplate and lovingly admire his likeness; and these can but awaken a painful longing for the original. He—the fair youth we love even in his more light-hearted moments, when among the whole retinue of the Graces he inhales from every flower the balsam breath of nature, the soul that they had breathed into it—has fled from the earth.* /

---

*The Occident has concocted for itself a quite different native spirit. His form shows its age—it was never particularly fair—and only a few faint traces of manliness remain. His father is bent with age; and he too is beyond even trying to look about joyfully or to rejoice in his own sense of well-being. Indeed he is so shortsighted that he doesn't have the courage to see any but the littlest things, one at a time. And lacking confidence in his powers, he never ventures anything bold. Iron fetters, cruel and (Ed. note: The remainder of this paragraph was evidently never completed and the extant portion was crossed out. —It is impossible to tell from the German syntax whether the 'he' in the phrase 'and he too is beyond' refers to the "native spirit" or to his father. Nor can this be definitively determined from the sense of the extant passage.]

Berne Fragments

(1793–94)

[1]¹

Aside from oral instruction, the influence of which is generally rather limited, extending only to those with whom we have close natural ties, the only way of achieving a large-scale effect is through writing. Here the educator stands on an invisible dais before the entire public; his invisibility provides him the opportunity to depict as vividly as he can the moral corruption of the public heart, which he addresses in a tone more unsparing than he would ever think to use toward even the most despicable individual. Indeed even when a moralist is impelled solely by the urgency of an inner devotion to the betterment of humankind rather than by his office, he is rarely seen to reproach the circle of people with whom he is on closer terms with even half the severity of what he directs at the respectable public at large. For this he lacks the nerve—and yet it is precisely from his more intimate circle that he must abstract the salient features of his broader critical portrayal; otherwise he is merely spouting drivel and prescribing remedies that are sheer theoretical quackery.

Generally, if one is to be successful in attempting to instruct a people, one has to take into account their distinctive frame of mind and take care to set the right tone; so also here [in the context of moral instruction] there are very different ways of going about things. Socrates, who lived in a republican state where every citizen spoke freely with every other and where a splendid urbanity of intercourse flourished even among the lowest orders, gave people a piece of his mind in the most natural manner imaginable. Without didactic tone, without the appearance of wanting to enlighten, he would start an ordinary conversation, then steer it in the most subtle fashion toward a lesson that taught itself spontaneously—one that would not seem obtrusive even to such as Diotima. The Jews on the other hand, in the tradition of their forefathers, were long accustomed to being ha-

---

1. This and the following fragment were apparently written in late 1793 or early 1794.

rangued in a far cruder fashion by their national poets. The synagogues had accustomed their ears to direct instruction and moral ser-
monizing, and the squabbles between scriptural authorities and the
Pharisees had inured them to a much coarser mode of / refuting one's
opponents. Hence to their ears a harangue that began "You serpents
and breed of vipers," delivered even by someone who wasn't a Pharisee or a Sadducee, sounded less harsh than it would have to Greek ears.

One would think that even if a person possessed the finest natural
endowments and had received the best of educations, he still couldn't
justifiably stop the lifelong effort of working on his intellectual and
moral perfection. So too with the less sophisticated yet enterprising
individual: given the sundry relationships he forms with others either
by accident or through his own initiative, since there is always something new to learn from them, he could never rest easy with himself
or even believe that he might. And this [recognition] seems all the
more compelling when we consider all the entangled relationships
characteristic of our civilized life, where even the most resolute uprightness may find itself caught up in a perplexing collision of duties,
such as when justice conflicts with the need for compassion in a specific instance, or when general principles of equity or, as is most common, prescriptive rights clash. Indeed here it is incumbent upon prudence to be all the more discreet; for we are never merely tending
to our own affairs but are ineluctably helping to further, on a large
or small scale, the well-being of a much greater mass of humanity.

This is why many a conscientious Nathanael[2] has preferred to place
himself outside of these relationships entirely, so as to spare himself
such perplexities and not have to do violence to his heart. For as relationships become more complex, so do the responsibilities; and as
they become less complex, so too are duties simpler. But ordinarily
it takes more effort to extricate oneself than never to get involved
in the first place—just as it is easier not to have certain needs to begin
with than to relinquish them voluntarily. Consider Diogenes: he was
by temperament disposed to make do with a swallow of water and
a piece of stale bread; his ambition was such that it did not take regal
purple to satisfy him—a torn coat would do. He had no pressing
obligations toward others as father or as friend, nor by virtue of his

2. The reference is apparently to Christ's disciple (see John 1:45–51). Cf. p. 62
below.

livelihood — aside from not beating them or (it can hardly have tempted him much) stealing from them. Diogenes made it easy for himself to be a perfectly moral man; indeed he has even earned a kind of right to be called a great man. At any rate perhaps he has time enough now to busy himself with others as well.

Among the Romans no Christ or Socrates rose forth; throughout the era of Rome's vitality, when only one virtue counted, no Roman could ever have been at a loss regarding what he had to do. There were only Romans in Rome, no humans; whereas in Greece the *studia humanitatis* / (of human sensibilities, of human inclinations and refinements) were highly prized. The Greeks allowed for many byways from nature which Socrates or some other sage might be inspired to retrace; but deviation from Roman nature was a crime against the state. For a people for whom the line demarcating perfection has thus been securely set down, for whom virtue is attached to something objective (in the service of which even raw passions can become virtues), it is generally rather easy to judge which kinds of action approach this line and which fall short of it. — But for a people who sense the urgency of a higher interest this is altogether more difficult to judge; amidst the press of conflicting duties, with human proclivities increasing along with responsibilities, it is infinitely more difficult to determine what exactly is virtuous and just how far nature should be subjected to reason.

[2]

Christ had twelve apostles, and this number stayed the same despite the fact that the number of his disciples was far larger. And the apostles alone enjoyed his intimate acquaintance, divesting themselves of all other ties in favor of his companionship and instruction, striving to become as totally like him as possible, and seeking to gain, by virtue of his teaching and living example, eventual possession of his spirit. How narrow-mindedly Jewish, how utterly worldly were their initial expectations, their hopes, their ideas. How slow they were to lift their gaze and their hearts from a Jewish messiah who would found an empire complete with generals and assorted high officials. How hard they found it to rise above the selfishness that always thinks of "me" first, and to enlarge their perspective to encompass the ambition of becoming mere fellow citizens of the kingdom of God. But Christ was not content to have disciples like Nathanael, Joseph of Arimathea, Nicodemus, and the like — to have had exchanges of ideas with men of exceptional intellect and heart — i.e. to have struck a few new ideas, a few sparks which, if they fall on material unsuitable for kindling, will be lost anyway. Men of this sort, while active and productive, are quite happy and content, come evening, in the bosom of their family; familiar with the world and its prejudices, they are tolerant of it, even while being quite hard on themselves: such men would never be receptive to the invitation to become a sort of adventurer.

Christ says that the kingdom of God does not manifest itself in outward appearances. It would seem, then, that his followers misunderstood his command: "Go all over the world, etc. and baptize them," at least insofar as they deemed baptism, this outward sign, to be universally necessary. This misunderstanding is all the more pernicious since discrimination by means of outward signs brings in its wake sectarianism and estrangement from others. Generally speaking, any distinction established on / moral grounds is undermined and begins to lose its power of illumination as soon as some other distinction is invoked. Christ says: "He who believeth thus and so. . . ." The text does not quite say: "He who believeth in me. . . ." It can be taken to imply the latter, but it does not have to, even though the apostles took it in this sense. Moreover, the shibboleths prevalent among their friends — the citizens of the kingdom of God — were not virtue and integrity, but Christ, baptism, etc. Had Christ not been so good a person . . . (see *Nathan*).[3]

Socrates, on the other hand, had disciples of all sorts — or rather he had none at all. He was merely a teacher and master, just as every individual who distinguishes himself by means of exemplary integrity and superior reason is a teacher for all. While he was bent on instruction, on enlightening and enlivening the people regarding matters that ought to awaken their most intense interest, one did not hear him speak *ex cathedra* or preach from a mountaintop — indeed, how could it ever have occurred to him to preach in Greece? He did not accept payment for his wisdom. And although there was nothing he might have wanted to achieve in this regard with his unsympathetic wife, he did not, for her sake, turn her out of doors, and thus

3. Lessing's *Nathan* again: II, 1.

33

maintained, without either repugnance or damage to his wisdom, his status as husband and father.

The number of his closer friends remained unspecified. The thirteenth, fourteenth, etc. was as welcome as the preceding, provided only that he was their equal in intellect and in heart. They were his friends, even his disciples—but in such a fashion that each remained what he was, without Socrates dwelling in each as the root from which they as branches obtained their vital fluids. He had no mold into which he wanted to pour his own qualities, no "rule" by means of which he sought to level out their differences—for this he certainly would have had enough paltry spirits at his disposal; but precisely these individuals, although freely admitted into his company, were never numbered among his more intimate friends. He had no interest in recruiting a small corps of men to serve as his bodyguard, all with the same uniform, the same drill, the same watchword—a group having but a single spirit and forever bearing his name.

And so although there were Socratics, there was never a Socratic guild such as the Masons, recognizable by their hammer and trowel; each of his pupils was a master in his own right, with many founding their own schools. A number of them became great generals, statesmen, heroes of all sorts—but not heroes of one and the same stamp, nor heroes in martyrdom and suffering; rather, each [prospered] in his own province of action and / life. Moreover, the fisherman remained a fisherman, and no one was to abandon house and home. Socrates began with each one's handicraft and led him from hand to spirit—from some subject matter with which each one was intimately acquainted and over which they could converse. From the soul of a given individual he developed concepts latent in it already and which needed nothing more than a midwife. He gave no one occasion to say: "What? Isn't this the son of Sophroniskus? Whence does he obtain such wisdom that he presumes to instruct us?"[4] He insulted no one by boasting of his own importance, or by using mysterious and lofty rhetoric capable of impressing only the ignorant and the gullible; among the Greeks, either would have made him an object of ridicule.

Just before he died—he died as a Greek, sacrificing a rooster to Aes-

34

---

4. A curious claim, in historical perspective. It is almost as if Hegel had not read Plato's *Apology*. But see note 16.

culapius, not as did Maupertuis, in a Capuchin cowl[5] — Socrates spoke with his disciples about the immortality of the soul. He spoke as would a Greek, appealing to the reason and imagination of his hearers, and with such animation — showing them what he hoped for so completely, intimately, and convincingly — that [it seemed to them that] they had been gathering the premises of this postulate all their lives. If so much could be vouchsafed us that such a hope would become a virtual certainty, it would contradict human nature and its spiritual capacities. But Socrates nonetheless so quickened this hope — for indeed the human spirit can, forgetting its mortal companions, rise above [its natural confines] — that it was almost as if he were a spirit from the grave who had climbed out and informed us concerning divine justice,[6] giving us more of an earful than the very tablets of Moses and all the oracles of the prophets carried in our hearts. And even if, contrary to the laws of human nature, such could really have taken place, Socrates would not have needed to fortify his comrades by means of a resurrection; only in impoverished spirits, within whom the premises of this hope (namely the idea of virtue and of the highest good) are not alive, is the hope of immortality so feeble.

Socrates left behind no Masonic signs, no mandate to proclaim his name, no method for seizing upon the soul and pouring morality into it: the *agathon*[7] is inborn in us; it is not something that can be drummed into us by preaching. He did not, in order to bring people to perfect goodness, outline some detour by way of *him* (a flowered path so fragrant that it assaults one's head);[8] he did not make himself the center and capital to which one journeys — laboriously, of course —

---

5. At this point in the text Hegel has the phrase: "—nicht wie ihr kommuniziert—". We find this so baffling that we are reluctant to render it in the text proper. Could Hegel be saying: "nor in the manner in which you [modern Christians] partake of it"? There are other possibilities, but they seem even more farfetched; e.g. "not in the garb in which he received the sacraments" (reading for the original: "nicht wie [er in] ihr Kommuniziert").

6. Cf. Schiller's "Resignation," 64–65.

> Kam je ein Leichnam aus der Gruft gestiegen,
> Der Meldung tat von der Vergelterin?
> [Did ever a corpse come climbing from the grave
> To give us news of divine justice?]

Cf. note 22 below.

7. the good

8. Cf. *Nathan*, III, 1.

only then to take / back home all sorts of provender most graciously   35
handed out and with interest to boot. He laid down no *ordinem salutis*
whereby every character, class, age, and temperament would have to
travel along a series of stations, through set stages of the soul and
of suffering. Instead, he knocked on the right door to begin with;
dispensing with mediators, he led the individual only into himself
without asking him to provide lodging for a guest, i.e. a spirit who
was a perfect stranger and who had arrived from some distant land.
No, he was asked merely to provide better light and room for this,
his old landlord, whom the mob of fiddlers and pipers had forced
to retreat into an old garret.

[3]⁹   36

The constitutions, legal codes, and religions of the various nations
bear the traces of their original childlike spirit even after it has long
since vanished. Power persists in the hands of an individual to whom
a "family" has naively entrusted its exercise as patriarch—even when
the nation is no more a family than the prince is a father. As soon
as their horizons had expanded somewhat, people began to feel that
in matters legal and constitutional their childlike trust was being abused,
prompting them to curb by means of specific laws the will, good
or bad, of their rulers. But in the various religions this childlike spirit
has lasted a good deal longer, and they continue to bear its traces
in countries where no benefits are expected from anyone beyond what
they are authorized or ordered to do.

This naive religious consciousness looks upon God as a mighty
lord, indeed with inclinations, passions, and even moods ("God rests").
Like the sovereigns among men, he does not always punish or provide prosperity in keeping with the rule of righteousness. One can
curry favor with him, and one tends to approach him in fear, or at
best in awe, rather than in love. And as has long been done with

9. Nohl: "This and the next three fragments, a sheet each and separated here
by a double skip, were placed under a single number because they somehow belong
together. The first two have no marking, the others are marked ⊐ and ⊋. In any case
a larger manuscript is missing here (cf. also the Appendix)." But see Harris 166n.
Harris and Schüler are persuaded that these fragments, though perhaps more closely
connected than Nohl thought they were, all date from 1794.

oriental potentates, and as the guileless still do with patrons and benefactors, one sacrifices to him a portion of the gifts (the happiness and
satisfaction) that nature bestows on mankind, culling one's first or
finest fruits as voluntary payment for whatever trust or joy one experiences. One imagines him nearer in one place rather than another,
and supposes that he would prefer to dwell among good and venerable
37   people, among the huts of the innocent / (like Baucis)[10] and find
such places and people more worthy of respect and more holy (*sem-
noi, pelorioi*).[11] To the childlike understanding it seems that the activity of God (or the gods) is most immediately manifest during storms,
floods, plagues, etc., in the surging of the sea and the menace of ava-
lanches; and indeed such an imagination attributes to him concern
with the affairs and circumstances of human life in general.*

This childlike consciousness has provided the impetus for religious
rites, customs, and representations (especially those having to do with
sacrifice, but also prayer and expiation) which reason often finds ridicu-
lous and bizarre, always deems unworthy, and indeed regards as utterly abominable when they are used by the power-hungry treacher-
ously to exploit the good faith of the people. Yet to this spirit itself
and to this sort of imagination fixated in childishness, these [repre-
sentations, etc.] often seem appealing, elevating, and at times profoundly moving. Sanctified and inculcated through tradition, with
the interests of so many people variously vested in them, this whole
nexus [of representations and practices], entwined as it is in universal custom, can be broken up only by the most extreme state of decay coupled with the advance of reason, and even then only amidst
violent convulsions. Nevertheless, as the spirit originally animating
these institutions gradually vanishes [*verfliegt*] so that the pious customs and exercises associated with them became burdensome in a way
not heretofore felt by the devout—and as reason makes steady headway
—such practices are indeed on the threshold of extinction. —But no
less incompatible with a rationality that demands effective dutiful
action is the kind of piousness that is wont to bring alms and sacrifices to the temples of the diety, unburden its heart through expiation, mortification, fasts, and long, intense prayer sessions, and

10. A poor and aged woman who, together with her husband Philemon, was
so hospitable to the disguised gods Zeus and Hermes that in gratitude they turned
her humble cottage into a temple.

11. Commonly translated: the revered, the mighty.

*God come down from heaven in order to see Sodom and Babel.

indulge in devout feelings of love and mystic sentiments. As reason presses forward, a lot of feelings are irretrievably lost, and many otherwise stirring associations in our imagination become more and more faint; yet we fondly associate such things with ethical simplicity, their depictions gladden and move us, and quite understandably we regret their loss.* Traces of them, hidden currents (quite aside from those linked with every human passion and inclination) continue to have their effect on us, and from time to time they surprise the individual who means to be perfectly rational with vestiges of his own humanness. Why else would people even to this day still enthusiastically hunt for, and sell dear, relics of Frederick the Great or Rousseau? /

It is these lingering impulses that draw us so strongly to, e.g., 38 portrayals of the age of chivalry, not just our regard for the valor and devotion depicted in them. And it is the tendency of the present age to confuse the disappearance of those once moving associations with the demise of ethical life as such that provokes its lamentations.

So long as this ethical simplicity is generally characteristic of a people—so long as everything sacred for the people as a whole is equally sacred for the princes and priests—we behold a spectacle incomparably stirring and salutary. Such is the good fortune that the South Sea Islanders enjoy, and perhaps the Peruvians as well before the conflict between Athahualpa and Huaskar. But as soon as a class (the rulers, the priests, or both) loses this spirit of innocence by which its laws and conventions were engendered and animated, then the general public will most certainly be oppressed, degraded, and demoralized, and ethical simplicity faces its inevitable doom. (This is why division into classes endangers freedom from the very start; for an esprit de corps is likely to emerge which soon becomes inimical to the spirit of the whole.) As soon as sacrifices and acts of atonement begin to be elicited from a people in a way differing from their long tradition, the collective whole ceases to be a community that approaches the altars of its gods in a fraternal spirit and with a sense of unanimity, and becomes rather a mass whose leaders coax from it pious sentiments which they themselves do not share. But unlike the magician, who elicits wonderment from a gaping crowd without himself finding anything remarkable, but also without any pretense of shar-

---

*the *lucus* [sacred wood] becomes a heap of lumber and the temple a pile of stones like any other; cf. Horace ep. I. 6, v. 31.

ing their amazement, these leaders—by their demeanor, their appearance, and their words—do in fact pretend to share such hallowed sentiments. For the silent spectator this contrast is all the more shocking the more he is moved by the simplicity and innocence of the multitude; the sight of a devout people, their eyes directed toward heaven, their hands pressed together, knees bent, and the sound of heavy sighs and ardent prayers would readily warm his heart with a pure and simple sentiment were it not for the bitter taste left by none other than the leading characters in this pageant.

How can a people tell whether their priests, even as they conduct divine services, have intentions other than that of bolstering piety, i.e. whether its confidence in them is not being abused?

The potential for this kind of corruption is due not only to the fact that the object of religion is something mysterious, but surely also to the fact that in most religions, the public ones in particular, some mysteries are exoteric while others are esoteric—so that therefore one had to have select qualities and special preparatory training in order to function as one of the trustees. And since these keepers were in closer proximity to the holy of holies than everybody else, a part of the reverence accorded it of course passed on to them. The latter were moreover charged with making the arrangements for the religious feasts (and for that matter, the national / festivals as well, which were presided over by the religious authority). Not only the collection but also the safekeeping or appropriation of the gifts offered to the deity were entrusted to their conscientious care.

Thus a people desiring to fashion a public worship that stirs heart, sense, and fantasy without leaving reason empty-handed—so that its devotion springs from the heightened, unified engagement of all the powers of the soul, so that its strict adherence to duty is portrayed as a gladder and more accessible task compatible with beauty and joy, and so that its pious sense of dependency on God not render it manipulable by a single class of men—will take care to manage its own feasts and itself oversee the use of the donations it collects. And if indigenous institutions engage its feeling, captivate its imagination, move its heart and satisfy its reason, then its spirit will feel no need—or rather it would no longer be content—to lend its ears every seven days to phrases and pictures which were intelligible and appropriate only several thousand years ago in Syria.

[4]

How little objective religion has accomplished on its own, without corresponding national and governmental institutions, is shown by its history since the rise of Christianity. How little has it been able to overcome the corruption of all classes, the barbarity of the times, or the crude prejudices of the common people. Opponents of the Christian religion, whose hearts were moved to pity for their fellow men by the history of the Crusades, the discovery of America, and the current slave trade, and whose hearts bled when, after reading of these shining events, they weighed the long chain of royal corruption and wholesale national decay in which the Christian religion has played such an outstanding role, even while its teachers and servants indulged in all sorts of declamations concerning the excellence and general usefulness of their services — these opponents must have been filled with a hatred so bitter that her defenders were prompted to ascribe to them a demonic malice of heart. In reaction to the brilliant and horrifying canvases on which the opponents of the Christian religion untiringly depict, with all the power of their brushes and all the acuity of their wit, the full extent of atrocities and miseries perpetrated by zealous commitment to some religion, the defenders rejoin that these weapons are out of date and that the arguments that can be pursued on this basis have long ago been refuted. In particular, however, they let their opponents know that all this mischief could have been avoided in the first place if only / mankind had at that time been fortunate   40 enough to have their moral compendia available.

But didn't the popes and their cardinals, didn't Cuckoopeter[12] and the priests of his time have Moses and the prophets? Were they unable to hear them? Didn't they have the same unpolluted source of morality that we still have today? Was morality in need of our paraphrasings, our learned systems? Was it somehow deficient? Was there something about it that — even if it could not tame the brutality of a people or change their customs for the better — kept it from having more of an effect on that very class of men whose life-work is moral knowledge and moral self-improvement? Was morality not of itself sufficient to restrain the lust for power manifest by the clergy in everything from their most shameless outrages to their little displays of

12. We have no idea who this refers to.

vileness—was it not sufficient for this class of men who display the badge of spiritual humility and who find their reward, the commendation of these virtues, daily in the teaching of the man to whom they allege to have dedicated their whole lives? Yet which of these vices was not expressly forbidden by their lord and master? Weren't the periods when princes were ruled by their father-confessors and the lands where spiritual lords ruled precisely the most wretched?

When placed in the balance, how light is the whole regimen of salvation, even when articulated in the fullest and most scholarly fashion! So what is the point of having all this crammed into one's head? When opposite it we drop onto the balance the weight of all the passions, the pressures of circumstance, education, example, and government, it will be flung high into the air.

Supposedly the chief design and accomplishment of the Christian religion is to better man morally and make him more pleasing to God. But before he can partake of the true religion, the true faith, he has to be either so pleasing to God that the true faith is spontaneously imparted to him, or so moral that he abhors evil and craves after righteousness—which is to say that through the Christian religion a person can become good if he was already good to begin with. Montesquieu [*The Spirit of the Laws*] (XXIV, ch. 2):

> To assemble a great tome listing at length the evils that have been perpetrated by religion, without doing the same with the good it has done, is to be altogether unfair. Were I to recount all the evils that have been generated in the world by civil laws, by monarchy, and by republican government, I would tell of frightful things! [13] /

41 If carried out only in keeping with the letter rather than the spirit— the spirit of virtue—many of the precepts Christ gave his disciples and hearers would be useless and even pernicious. So too, the legal code of a state where ethical custom holds sway more so than the laws would be inadequate and useless in a state where literally anything is permissible if not expressly forbidden by law. Thus many of Christ's precepts are contrary to the foundational principles of legislation (the principles governing the rights of property, self-defense, etc.) in civil societies. Were a nation to introduce Christ's precepts

---

13. Hegel quotes this in the original French. The translation is ours.

today—ordering at best external compliance with them, since the spirit cannot be effectively commanded—it would very quickly come apart. No one has ever heard of somebody who, having had his coat stolen but managing to keep his vest and trousers, was scolded by a Christian teacher for not having surrendered the latter as well. Likewise with oath-taking: the clergy performs a most solemn role here, although it must surely be aware that Christ expressly forbade it.

So what aroused the hatred of the Jewish scribes and councilors most of all against Christ? Was it not the singular manner in which he both acted in his own right and judged the actions of others, one that not only offended their sacred customs but violated their civil laws? When the question arose as to how a case was to be judged in accordance with judicial laws, Christ attacked the administrators of these laws. But even assuming they had been the most blameless of men and entirely of Christ's mind, they would still have had to pass sentence not accordingly, but in keeping with the laws. There are times when the judge must speak differently from the human being; the former must often condemn what the latter excuses.

What all this means is that the teachings of Jesus, his rules of conduct, were really suited only for the cultivation of singular individuals, and were oriented accordingly. Consider for example the young man who asks him: "Master, what shall I do to attain perfection?" and is told to sell all he owns and give the proceeds to the poor. When we imagine this being put into effect as a rule of conduct for even a small community or humble village, it yields consequences so absurd that we cannot conceive its extension to a larger populace. Suppose that a community like that of the first Christians banded together in the midst of another people under such a law of communal property. The spirit of such a law would vanish in the very instant of its establishment. A kind of pressure would well up generating an atmosphere of concealment (as happened to Ananias).[14] / And the charitableness associated with this sort of resignation would tend to focus only on fellow members, on those who have likewise adopted these customs and bear the marks of membership—a situation inimical to the spirit of charity, which pours its blessings upon circumcised and uncircumcised, baptized and unbaptized alike.

42

---

14. Ananias fell dead when Peter reproached him for withholding from the apostles the proceeds of some land he had sold (Acts 5: 1–10).

[5]

. . .[15] public authority, presuming to force its way into the sanctuary of the heart, to which one spontaneously grants access only to one's friend. At this point it begins fabricating an account of [human] intentions and motives ad hoc.

Little by little this arrogant practice of prying into a person's innards, of judging and punishing his conscience, began insinuating itself [in Christian society], and did so without much difficulty, since the germ of this presumptuous attitude — its tendency falsely to extend what is appropriate only in the context of the immediate family to civil society as a whole — lay within Christianity from its very inception. It became incredibly deep-rooted (it must seem incredible that people should forget their rights on such a scale while hardly sensing the loss) and burgeoned into the most shocking profusion of repressive institutions and ways of deluding mankind: oral confession, excommunication, penances, and a whole array of disgraceful monuments to human self-abasement. Then the reformers, intent upon patterning their principles of conduct on the maxims of the New Testament and meaning to reproduce — by setting up Christian magistracies (ecclesiastical police) — the unity and uniformity of the earliest church, were misled [by their own efforts] into losing sight of the difference between measures requisite for a folk religion to gain ascendancy and the sort of regulations appropriate only for an exclusive group or a private organization. It never occurred to them that they might establish an ecclesiastical authority as a bastion of freedom of conscience to counterbalance princely authority — indeed they made Christianity subservient to princely power. Yet how, really, could they ever have liberated themselves from the conception of the church as a kind of *status in statu,* the idea of a uniform community visible to all, and severed their bonds with this defined body of religious custom? Just how far Luther, for example, was from the idea of worshiping God in spirit and truth was made clear by his wretched disputes with Zwingli, Oekolampad, etc. Although he did strip the clergy of their power to rule by force and to control the purse, he still wanted to retain control over men's thoughts. At the same time the princes and court clergy, these guardians of the people, gave their spiritual

15. Some text missing here.

children stewards who were to lead them by the hand, admonish them, and when necessary discipline them with the rod. Hence ecclesiastical punishments (church-imposed penances, confession, etc.) were retained alongside political ones; and although oral confession in the strict sense / was abolished, we still had priests as father-confessors. 43 —All this was done in order to come to the aid of a troubled conscience made anxious to begin with by relentless assaults on its imagination. Religion was supposed to consist once again simply of improvement of the heart, repentance, and conversion. But of course it wasn't enough to have only these rather general ways of giving expression to our spirituality (which in fact varies from heart to heart, depending on temperament, disposition, and the bent of one's imagination). Individual states of spirit had to be dissected and the inner play of feelings tampered with; they had to be put on display as though they were so palpable and perceptible that one could know their genesis and presence as easily as one can look at a clock to see if it is twelve. Made out as though they were the same in everybody, these states were meticulously described in portrayals devoid of any real knowledge of the human heart, pieced together artificially from assorted theological prejudices alleging the innate depravity of human nature, and arranged in accordance with an exegesis laughably bereft of psychological insight. With this the conscience and memory of the common man were relentlessly hounded and flattered, until this pasty mix of sweetness and bitterness ruined his health, strength, and vitality. Perforce he was now disposed to misunderstand his own impulses and inclinations in countless ways; undermined by his own tremulous conscience, the very integrity of his sensibility was compromised by all this indigestible verbiage and replaced by a vapid sentimentality. What had once been vital energy, self-reliance, and self-respect now became hypocritical meekness: a spiritual vanity forever preoccupied with itself and its impulses, endlessly chattering about its feelings and its triumphs over fearful temptations.

By this time the clergy had its hands full clearing away people's doubts, warding off their temptations, alerting them to the clandestine powers of evil, and offering solace for suffering brought on by the world, the temptations of Satan, and their own evil aspirations and desires. We find sufferers who can no longer tolerate healthy air and fresh water, and who have come to live on insipid broths and pharmaceutical concoctions; every wind that presses on their innards, every sneeze, every clearing of the throat is entered in their diary. Preoccupied as they are with no one more than themselves, the most they will do for a fellow suppliant is offer one of their home remedies and commend him to God's care. And the theological compendia they use are all of a piece: although they do not consist of actual religious insights but rather of what is supposed to give knowledge of psychological processes and evoke certain emotive states, they profess to be

44   wholly / in line with the guiding principle that repentance and conversion are what matter most. Yet one is taken on the most unexpected detours, so that it comes as no surprise when one finds oneself entirely too distracted to arrive at a true and lasting goal.

This conception of betterment and the way leading to it is so convoluted, divided into so many waystations, and outfitted with so much unfamiliar nomenclature (it does express a single subject matter, but one so strange and complicated that it seems to have God knows what mysterious and portentous content, ranging from the *gratia applicatrix* to the *unio mystica*) that one can no longer recognize in it the simplest things. When one looks at these things in broad daylight and with healthy eyes, one cannot help but be embarrassed at so much art and erudition being expended on something it takes common sense a quarter of an hour to grasp.

In our day we have discovered that subjective religion is resistant to dogma, and that dogma has by and large been relegated to the province of objective religion where it provides doctrines that, although not always adapted to reason, do help to exercise our memory and understanding. But this ecclesiastical discipline of the Christians is not something that first got started on its own and then was introduced as a new idea in the statutes of Christian society; as we have seen, it was already inherent in Christianity in its earliest and crudest conception—having thereafter merely been exploited and expanded by hypocrisy and the lust for power. —However much the traces of the crudest abuse of this discipline may have begun to fade, its spirit survives to an incalculable degree. We have here yet another illustration of the fact that the institutions and laws of a small society (whose every citizen retains the freedom to be or not to be a member),[16]

16. Hegel could conceivably be thinking here of Socrates in Plato's *Apology.* But in that form the idea would not be too convincing as a generalization in cultural anthropology.

when expanded to encompass civil society at large, are no longer appropriate and cannot coexist with civil liberty.

[6]

Imagine a community in which the citizen is not automatically expected to defend his fatherland, but which does have enough volunteers willing to take on this responsiblity for money. Here, conceivably, a group of individuals could bind themselves never to take up arms, abstaining from all wars, accepting neither their legitimacy nor the profits that accrue as the result of continual triumph. They might genuinely believe that they are under no circumstances justified in seeking the death of other human beings. And they might even counter single acts of violence with nothing but patience and submissiveness. But were such a group to expand into a state in its own right, it could never retain its principles in their universality—at least not without risking, contrary to every natural impulse, the complete surrender of the prosperity and well-being of a whole people to the insolence of a handful of brigands. /

The best education for children is the good example they see around 45 them every day. The more one has to order them about, the more they are inclined to disobedience and sullen obstinacy. The same holds true for the education of mankind at large. They dread and shun (*ils ne se pretent pas, ils se refusent*)[17] any religion that would always be trying to lead them around by the hand like children, that would talk down to them about any number of virtues and vices that, having been portrayed only *in abstracto,* they have never encountered in real life and so might be totally irrelevant to actual human circumstances. On the other hand, without their knowing it, people are under the secret influence of—and even the freest of individuals is dependent upon—the attitude of the people around them. No matter how intolerant people are of moral reproach, if one preaches virtue, repentance, and atonement to them in a merely general way, each takes it to heart and to some extent accepts what is said because it concerns everyone and not just himself. But if one's depiction of prevalent vices is exact and at the same time somewhat specific, the effect

17. They do not give themselves to it; they resist it.

it has on anyone who feels it aimed at him, as an attack on *his* wealth or mode of conduct, is more likely to be embitterment; for surely he doesn't regard any authority as being entitled to such presumption. (While children are ruled by sheer sensuousness, by love and fear, a mature person is in addition susceptible to the guidance of reason; hence, unlike a child, he finds it difficult to do something for someone out of affection, or even to act in his own best interest, without first determining whether this is a good thing to do.) Everyone finds strangers insufferable when they meddle in their affairs, especially when they begin interfering with the way they do things. But most insufferable are the publicly installed custodians of morals. Anyone who acts with a pure heart will be the first to be misunderstood by these assessors of everything moral and religious.

[7]

Concerning Variations in the Way Death is Depicted

The entire life of the Christian is supposed to prepare him for this transformation; and indeed his every hope and expectation is oriented in this direction. Daily commerce with depictions of death and hopes for the life beyond—in contrast with which the pleasures and joys of this world, to which he does not become very attached and in which, like a stranger, he takes only a passing interest—are supposed to make his departure from this, the arena of his activity, not only less terrifying but in a sense actually agreeable. Diminished as his anxiety concerning the moment of death may be, he worries even less about his impending destiny / or about the prospect of annihilation, the utter termination of the harmonies once the instrument is broken. His whole life has been a *meditatio mortis.* To him the world is but a preparatory school for the future; it has no inherent worth but only an instrumental value in connection with what is to come. What, after all, is an expenditure or investment of a mere fifty to eighty years which, when measured against boundless eternity (the full duration of our existence), are but an instant? —And yet who in a mere sixty years could forget, even for a moment, the frightful alternative: eternal bliss—or eternal damnation? Who would not, in view of this incessant arousal of his fears that he may be unworthy of eternal happiness, fly toward the means of grace tendered by the doctrine that introduces these terrors? At this frightful and catastrophic moment,

at which one not only takes leave from everything he once held dear—
in a matter of mere hours or minutes to never again behold the light
of the sun, but rather see looming before him the throne of judgment
before which his destiny will be decided for all eternity—at this moment of anxious expectation, who would not surround himself with
all the instruments of solace at his disposal? This is why we see the
beds of the sick surrounded by clergymen and friends groaning forth
the printed and prescribed sighs over the anxiety-ridden soul of the
dying one. This is why we hear the refrain *memento mori* terminating
every admonition and exhortation—the most compelling incentives
to action being fetched from beyond the grave. Dying well, i.e. piously,
consists in retaining sufficient presence of mind to remember the passages and chants one had to memorize with such effort in school,
and to recite them now along with other things.

The heroes of nations die in much the same way as they have lived;
they in the course of their lives have learned to appreciate the power
of nature. On the other hand those who find nature's lesser evils intolerable eventually become incapable of enduring its larger consequences. If this is not so, how is it that a people whose religion makes
preparation for death into a cardinal point, a cornerstone of the entire
edifice, tend to die in so unmanly a fashion—while people of other
nations calmly await the arrival of this moment? —We are all familiar
with the individual who, in anticipation of a dinner party, starts early
in the morning by having his hair curled, preoccupying himself with
laying out all his fanciest clothes, ordering his horses hitched up to
his carriage, and, totally consumed with the importance of the impending party, spends all day pondering over how he will act and
where he will steer the conversation—as though he were a young
orator anxious as to whether he will put on a / good enough show.*   47
By contrast we have the individual who spends the morning tending
to his affairs, remembers his engagement a few minutes before the
dinner hour, and goes off to it calmly and casually as though he were
still at home. —How different were the pictures of death implanted
in the Greek imagination from the ones our people harbor: among
them it was a beautiful spirit, the brother of Sleep, immortalized in
the monuments above their graves; among us it is Death, whose gruesome skull hovers over all our coffins. For them death was a reminder

---

*Among the pious people the affectation of disdaining the good things of life
is commonplace—[these evoke a] grimace.

of the joy of living—to us it is cause somehow to endure it; for them death bore the scent of life—to us it just smells like death. They euphemized death, moderating their depictions of it, but we, when in respectable society, altogether avoid speaking or writing of this natural thing, while our orators and preachers, determined to strike terror in us and spoil our pleasure, paint death in the most hideous colors available. /

48

[8]

[a schematic outline][18]

α) By *objective* religion I understand the entire system in which our duties and aspirations are interconnected with the idea of God and of the immortality of the soul. Thus when the concern of objective religion is not merely knowledge of the existence and attributes of God as such but rather what all this has to do with mankind and the requirements of human reason, it may still be called theology.

β) To the extent that such a theory doesn't just exist in books but in concepts that people actually grasp, i.e. to the extent that love of duty and respect for the moral law are strengthened by a [comprehensive] idea and are more deeply felt, we have *subjective* religion. —Now since civil legislation has legality rather than morality as its immediate objective, and since there are no institutions specifically intended to promote respect for the moral law and the disposition to fulfill it in keeping with its spirit (moral concerns generally being regarded as proper to religion), we are not inclined to dissociate religion and morality, but on the contrary consider the latter to be the

18. Nohl comments: "The three fragments that follow—outlines of a critique of Christianity—belong together as outline, initial sketch, and more fully developed draft. The sketch consists of one-half sheet. The two other pieces (four + three sheets) Hegel himself numbered 1–7, and at two points he makes reference to these numbers; this has been replaced with our pagination. Hegel's lettering in the sketch became so convoluted and confusing that it had to be altered. In the margin there is this scheme (once again somewhat altered further down): A. Introduction. B. (a) doctrines; b) traditions; c) ceremonies; d) public religion. . . ." Harris has his doubts about the sequence and connectedness of these fragments (see e.g., 183n), but not about their being written in 1794 (see 520). Cf. note 20 below. What Nohl calls the "initial sketch" begins on p. 80 below, the "more fully developed draft" on p. 92. The subtitles on pp. 81 and 90 are to be found in the margins of Hegel's manuscript.

primary purpose of religious institutions — not something it merely
promotes by means of the idea of God.

γ) Not all the driving impulses in human nature — reproduction,
for instance — have morality as their purpose; still, man's highest purpose is morality, and among the various natural tendencies that promote it, man's religious instinct is one of the most important. By
its very nature our awareness [*Erkenntnis*] of God cannot be dead:
it has its source in man's moral nature, in practical needs — and out
of it in turn morality / springs. — Or is the propagation of the name   49
and fame of Christ, or of Mohammed, to be taken as the main purpose of religion? If it were, then in the Grecian world Orpheus and
Homer would have deserved just as much renown and respect as Jupiter and Pallas. Religion would then have good cause to be proudest
of Karl, converter of the Saxons, or of the proselytizing Spaniards
in America, or even of the Jew-hunter Schulz. — Or is religion supposed to be the glorification of God's name? In that case there would
be no better Christians than the song-filled swallows of St. Bridget.
Indeed then the pope celebrating high mass in St. Peter's would be
a worthier object of God's good will than the corporal (Woltemar)[19]
who risked his life in service of his fellow man, saving thirteen persons during a shipwreck, and dying to save a fourteenth.

δ) Making objective religion subjective: this great undertaking the
state must assume. To this end its institutions must be compatible
with freedom of conviction; they must not violate conscience and
liberty, but exert only an indirect influence on the motives of the
will. How much can the state [properly] do? And how much must
be left up to each individual?

ε) Religion attains this objective, the advancement of morality,
through (a) its *teachings* and (b) its *ceremonies*, to which every religion, in keeping with its natural interests, has been carefully attentive. And the state plays a role in this through its constitution, the
animating spirit of the government.

ζ) To what extent does the Christian religion prove to be suitable
for this purpose? The Christian religion was originally a private religion, but was modified as required by the conditions under which
it came into being, the people it had to deal with, and the prejudices
confronting it.

a) The (α) practical teachings of the Christian religion are

19. *Woltemar* was a much discussed novel by F. H. Jacobi (1743–1819).

[morally] pure and have the additional advantage of being on the whole set forth in examples. In cases where (Matthew 5, 6, etc.) the spirit of morality is set forth only in general terms and, instead of being limited to formal principle, includes material precepts, it is susceptible to misunderstanding and indeed has been misunderstood. (β) With regard to the historical truths on which this religion is founded, their miraculous aspect is always subject to disbelief. To the extent that Christianity is a private religion, everyone is free either to believe or not; but to the extent that it becomes public, nonbelievers are inevitable. (γ)[20] So long as no provision is made for the imagination (contrary to the Greek practice), the Christian religion remains a dreary and melancholy affair— something oriental, neither grown in our own soil nor readily assimilable.

b) Ceremonies that were appropriate enough when religion was private lose their sense and spirit completely by the time it becomes public—quite aside from the fact that then, even in their role as instruments of grace, they have no close bond with the spirit of joy. Such ceremonies could nonetheless, having become public, also have become means of promoting tolerance, had they not at the same time been forcibly tied to divisive / presuppositions. By now, alas, they have become sectarian signatures—the very opposite of what they might have been.

c) Other requirements pertaining to religious life: (1) Distantiation from public affairs (2) Distribution of alms—the collection of a public fund for this purpose is possible in a private religion, but is not feasible within the state; what was once an act of piety is now bound up with public honor.

[9]

a)[21] It would seem to be no easy matter to construct a system of religious and moral truths that can win the free assent of all or even

---

20. Here Hegel's manuscript actually has a gimel, the third letter of the Hebrew alphabet; and under item c) below has a) and b) rather than 1) and 2)

21. There is no b) forthcoming.

most people, since we consider it absolutely essential that a folk religion's doctrines not be obtrusive or repressive of anyone's conscience. Indeed we would appear to have enough of a task on our hands were we even to give quick consideration to the plethora of already existing systems and hypotheses worked out by philosophers and theologians ever since human reason matured to the point that it could actually have ideas and engage in speculation concerning them. But inasmuch as we are aware of the sheer variety of possible religious and moral representations, and realize that, no matter how bizarre these may seem to us, they always find disciples once they've been linked to common human needs and ideas — and inasmuch as we know from experience that a people's freedom of conscience can be impaired and a dangerous fanaticism kindled in them when any of these representations is promoted by public decree or proscription — it should be apparent to us that the tenets of a folk religion should as a rule be as simple as possible. That is to say, they should contain nothing which common human reason does not acknowledge — no specific, dogmatic assertions that might overstep the bounds of reason, even if their authority is alleged to derive from heaven itself.

Mysterious theoretical doctrines

As a matter of course [religious and moral] teachings of this sort run the risk of being adopted by reason and so exposed to attack; and it is quite possible that some unripe fruit may be knocked off, crushed, and smothered. But as the ripening process continues, neither bonfires for authors (or at least their books) nor symbolic acts of exorcism can check this "evil" whose seed is ineradicably planted in human nature. For reason leads us irresistably to the great principle that duty and virtue are self-sufficient — a principle whose sanctity is surely being undermined when the motives calling for duty and virtue are any more circuitous or heterogeneous than the merest association / with the idea of God; hence, when some fantastic doctrine is deemed 51 by the devotees of reason to be morally innocuous even though it is favorable to despotism, they are not prepared to do any more than acknowledge its role in restraining the vulgar rabble. Convinced that reason in its very essence is identical with their faith in rationalism, each in his own way is determined to render powerless those who oppose this faith: one challenges positive religion by invoking its own principles and the arguments contained in its own texts; another uses the weapons of wit; and still another, convinced that these positive doctrines are sanctified in the faith of the people even though they are actually quite meaningless for him personally, tries to accommodate his ideas to them. And among the many who have developed the idea of morality solely out of their own hearts, who have beheld her beauty as though in a mirror and become enchanted by her, whose souls have rendered highest tribute to virtue and moral greatness—a Spinoza, a Shaftesbury, a Rousseau, a Kant—we find that the more these men came to revere morality and the moral character of Christ's teaching, the more did everything else appear irrelevant and superfluous.

Arcane, incomprehensible dogmas—precisely because they are incomprehensible—can no more be represented in reason or in the understanding than they can be portrayed in the imagination, whose function they totally contradict.* When faced with doctrines of this sort, all three [of these faculties] must suspend operation and put up with a temporary cessation of their activity, since here the laws that govern them are as useless as if one were to measure wine with a yardstick or try to caricaturize someone by using the head of Apollo. Thus all that we have left to deal with them is memory, which then has to assimilate certain word combinations and store them away in a place of their own, as far removed from the understanding as possible.

But the chief function of these incomprehensible doctrines has yet to be considered, namely what bearing do they have on the heart: what practical claims do they make on a person, what incentives do they provide, what hopes do they offer one? A good number of these doctrines are such that essentially they have no practical force, except when combined with other doctrines that do. —But in any case all of these doctrines must adhere to the fundamental law that they endorse no way of pleasing God other than a good life, and advocate 52   no motives to morally good conduct / other than purely moral ones. Still, when religion promotes this concept of being pleasing to God, there is considerable variation in the purity of the meaning. Indeed, between our endeavor to stand upright before God, our ideal of holiness, and our desire for exclusive and special favor in his sight because

---

*The objective truth and validity of such doctrines is not at all at issue here, but rather what they, even if they are proven to be true, constitute for our reason, for our imagination, and for our heart.

of our performance of some sensuous practice, there is a whole spectrum of attitudes that are never sufficiently sorted out or focused upon.

Therefore, since the concept of being pleasing to God, which religion advances as its highest aim, is so susceptible to impure formulations, religion must conscientiously protect it from the encroachment of any representation harmful to its practice.

Actually there is an implicit contradiction in the demand that doctrines transcending reason and imagination, when applied to practical matters, ought to show us no way other than a good life and no other means of becoming pleasing to God. For if these doctrines did not show us a new way, they would hardly be incomprehensible or for that matter be mysteries. Such teachings generally demand only that we perform certain exercises in order to be pleasing to the Divine Being (some of these are oral, while others involve our hands and feet; some elicit a whole Glockenspiel of feelings, while others entail renunciation or even chastisement of the flesh; and some just involve our believing certain things). This is how we are supposed to be exempted or granted special dispensation from the moral law. —But reason has to brush away these webs of dogma even though they be attested to by the most sacred seals in the faith of nations and ages. In its demand that we be morally good, reason can make no concessions.

The history of all eras teaches us how corrupt are those states (or at least some of their constituent classes) where rules of conduct like these have prevailed, where all natural relations have been perverted by such immoral religious balderdash. The same lesson is being taught to this very day by the dismal picture of states where these systems still prevail, for instance in the Pontifical State or in Naples. Only the basic goodness of human nature, which can never be entirely stamped out (although here it is admittedly in rather bad shape), coupled with the fact that in time of crisis civil legislation of necessity modifies the rules of conduct in some respects in order for society to survive, prevent our vices and vicious tendencies from forming a seamless web with doctrines that have come to nourish, justify, and exculpate them.

I include here such publicly authorized beliefs as these: that by attending masses and by obtaining indulgences one can not only buy off his sins but be inferior in goodness to no one; that in the public eye / corporal as distinguished from other forms of punishment are   53 dependent on differences [in social status]; that the interpreters of the divine will may remove criminals from the arm of justice and provide them sanctuary; that it is more fitting, not just on the basis of [individual] belief but as a matter of public policy, that the beggar is to be favored even when the hard-working man fares ill. —But we are not referring here simply to the doctrines of a few sophists or empirics whose philosophical acuteness is such that they could never accept *any* principle that might define virtue and vice, nor to the activities of a few libertines whose lives have never been in the least complicated by concern with principles and whose passions have made them deaf to the voice of virtue: such eccentrics, however common, are not our concern. Rather, we are talking about principles which literally pervert morality at the same time that they debase both humanity and divinity—not the sort of principles that are debated by the effete in studies and lecture halls, where without perceptible harm to the public welfare one professor espouses happiness and another some other empirical commonplace as the basis of morality or natural right. These are not simply given out in public instruction, but, more effectively communicated than any lecture, they are insinuated throughout the entire complex of a nation's activity. In such states (in addition to a few individuals who will in no way allow themselves to travel the openly sanctioned highway of degradation and vice) there are some who, at least sensing that sounder principles are needed, strike a compromise between their own better sense and the prevalent principles through devices like the above—an amalgamation so flimsy that they have to hide it from their own intelligence, even if it does serve to assuage the heart.

Such doctrines must therefore be absolutely repudiated by reason, regardless of whether they are rules of conduct for private individuals or, applied more generally, for the management of an entire state. —Be that as it may, precisely these positive religious doctrines, which could hardly have turned up in the course of reason's own development, are alleged to have a better purpose; and especially in recent times the practical aspect of all the dogmatic teachings has been strenuously sought out and cultivated.

There has been a retreat from efforts to make the mysteries of religion acceptable by means of reason. Much stock is now placed in the distinction that although said doctrines transcend reason, they are not contrary to it—a distinction which does indicate a certain timid regard for reason, a certain measure of respect for its authority, but which in the end isn't worth much. For if reason is the highest judge / of its own belief, it will neither accept nor believe what it will not plausibly encounter or be able to apply anywhere in its endeavors.* In this regard reason is rather like the geographer who, having discovered no northwest passage through America despite all his efforts, has the audacity to declare that there is none.

Such verbiage, which is wasted on reason because she cannot comprehend it—which the understanding cannot grasp and imagination cannot depict, and which can at best be mulled over by memory—can thus have no importance for man except in so far as it affects the heart's role in the determination of the will.

It is undeniable that in several respects the Christian doctrine of things transcending the human does not actually have morality but rather mere legality as its purpose and consequence. To be sure, these can be refined and redirected so as to become moral doctrines; but until prodded by the objections and reproaches of opponents, no one had been too eager to make the attempt. For a long, long time they were really used only

> To storm the imagination of the dreamer
> When the torch of the law burns but dimly[22]

arousing the hope that by some supernatural means morality will be realized—or the fear that some supernatural means could make things worse. I need only refer to the representations of all sorts of rewards (e.g. mystical bliss, which rests on childish, frivolous, or even immoral pride), or to the even more evocative, graphic, and sensuous depictions of punishments, e.g. the torments of hell, where with unflagging inventiveness the devil torments souls for ever and ever and without hope of salvation. As one need hardly wonder, many an imagination, subjected to the force of these representations, has become unhinged; many people have been driven to despair and indeed to madness.

If the Greek priestesses of Bacchus became so enfrenzied that they imagined themselves face to face with divinity and gave themselves over to the wildest excesses of drunkenness, theirs was a joyous, jubi-

---

*One could say that these dogmas are not inherently contrary to reason, but it is contrary to reason to believe them.

22. From a stanza (later suppressed) of Schiller's "Resignation" (cf. note 6 above).

lant rapture — an enthusiasm that easily carried over into ordinary life. But the extravagances of the modern religious imagination lead to eruptions of the most dismal and anxiety-ridden despondency, leav-
55 ing one's organs / devastated and frequently beyond repair. Dogma as we know it provides not merely the doctrine but the specifics, the closer details of depictions like the above. And all that is entrusted to the more or less lively imagination of the teacher is their illustration in a vividly gruesome fashion.

The expectation of rewards and punishments in another world is so naturally grounded in reason's practical need to establish some connection between this and another life that this doctrine has been a preeminent feature of all religions. But in order to be worthy of a moral religion and to obtain a secure foothold in the faith of the various peoples, it must be handled with considerable care. — But we are not ready to consider what cultivating and refining the imagination would entail in this context; rather, we are still focusing on Christian religious teachings to the extent that they are based on principles that transcend reason — and this in spite of the fact that belief in what the imagination depicts is demanded as though it too were dogma. The doctrine of the resurrection of the body, for instance, has no great moral import; its only effect (which in itself was morally insignificant) was to prevent the concept of the human soul as a spiritual and incorporeal essence from becoming more universal. Religious hope, having no idea of an incorporeal, incorruptible, immortal essence while at the same time trusting in the continuation of personal existence (against which death, the extinction of that existence, speaks so naturally), had resorted to allowing the revival of the notion that the body is not merely one's intimate companion but in fact one's very self.

Our hope that we will be compensated for all the suffering we endure is such a comforting thought — and we demand this in the name of justice. Still we are forced to accustom ourselves to the fact that not everything that goes counter to our expectations can be seen as an injustice, and we would do well to get used to regarding ourselves as more dependent on nature [than we are willing to admit]. The complexity of our political and civil relationships, the diversity of our modes of life, and the inequality of our share of earthly goods have not only multiplied miseries of every kind but have also increased our sensitivity and susceptibility to them. The suffering to which we are exposed by our nature as well as our manner of life (which so often deviates from nature), is quite commonly accompanied by an intolerant impatience stemming from our demand that everything should go well for us and in accordance with our wishes, and our belief that every misfortune is an injustice.

Behind the alleged contempt for the goods and honors of this world what we often find instead is envy of those who possess them. But often this contempt turns out to be frustration; that one must do without / these things is then regarded as an injustice, as suffering   56 for which, once again, compensation is due. On the other hand there are many who, convinced that our sufferings in this world are not sufficient exchange for the splendors of the one to come, actually believe that without suffering they could in no way partake of the latter. Afforded a peaceful enjoyment of this life in keeping with a fulfillment of its obligations, they nonetheless live not only full of vigilance concerning their virtue but in actuality full of apprehensiveness. They provide themselves with a vast array of real and imaginary miseries, and complain about this world being a vale of tears when in fact they have nothing to bemoan.* —All such dispositions lead away from the spirit—the truth—of any would-be moral connection between this life and the one to come.

A doctrine peculiar to Christianity—and one quite alien to reason—is the dreadful alternative alleged to be the eventual fate of mankind in the other world: either eternal bliss or eternal damnation, there being nothing in between. Now, were people's representations of an afterlife as secure and reliable as even their certainty that quinine is a cure for fever, such an alternative would leave one without a moment's peace in this life, since after it the dispensation of grace summarily ends while that of inexorable justice commences. Indeed one would be thrown into a state of the most tortured uncertainty and, painfully conscious of imperfection, would be endlessly vacillating between terror before the universal Judge and hope in a merciful and forgiving Father. An excruciating state indeed—albeit one that isn't too commonly experienced, if only because humankind is so inconsistent when it comes to rules of conduct not based on anything found in its own nature but merely pounded into the head from without.

---

*Our savants, when they are not favorably reviewed, complain of suffering the slings of outrageous fortune.

Of enormous practical significance here is the story of [the life of] Jesus, and not just what he taught or is alleged to have taught. To love goodness, to do what is right in the right way, to love virtue of one's own free choice rather than merely appear to do so because of fleeting impulses in this direction—all this requires principles, a predominance of metaphysics over physics, of abstract ideas over sensuous ones. When will humankind have come far enough that principles predominate over feelings, laws over individuals? If virtue, said Plato, were to appear visibly among men, then / all mortals would have to love it. He did of course believe in virtuous individuals; but in order that people be moved to appreciate and emulate virtue, he demanded virtue itself. Now the story of Jesus is not simply about a man who, having prepared for the task by educating himself in solitude, devoted his allotted time exclusively to the betterment of mankind, eventually sacrificing even his life to this end. Were nothing more at stake, then Socrates (to cite the most familiar example) would do equally well as mirror and model. After all, he drew his wisdom from the tumult of an active life that included battles in which he saved the life of a friend while risking his own. And he devoted himself to the improvement of his fellow citizens until at last Truth handed him the poisoned cup, which he emptied with the utmost composure. —What would we lack if we took Socrates as our exemplar of virtue? Wasn't Socrates a man with powers not exceeding our own? Could we not undertake to imitate him, confident that in the course of our lives we can attain his level of perfection? By contrast, what did Christ's help to the sick cost him, aside from a few words? Endowed with a divine power that cannot be in the least affected or swayed by sensuality and that cannot be impeded for lack of means and resources, might not Jesus, with his irreproachable life, his steadfastness, his silence in suffering, strike us as so completely wondrous that instead of being moved to imitate him, we are left without hope of ever attaining to such ourselves? —Be that as it may, when our understanding coldly pursues such a line of reasoning, our imagination simply pays no heed. It is precisely the admixture, the addition of the divine, that makes the virtuous individual Jesus fit to be an ideal of virtue. Without the divinity of his person we would have only the man; whereas here we have a truly superhuman ideal—an ideal not foreign to the human soul, however short of it humankind might be compelled to regard itself. Moreover, an ideal like this has the advantage of not being a frigid abstraction: already akin to our spirit, it is brought still closer to us by its individualization for our sensibility (our hearing it speak and seeing it act). Hence, what is now manifest to the believer is not just a man who is virtuous but Virtue itself; with a mere virtuous man we are always inclined to assume hidden shadows, signs of struggles past (if only, as in the case of Socrates, on physiognomic grounds). Whereas here faith is in the presence of a virtue that is flawless yet not disembodied.

The added dimension of the divine in Jesus, which on the face of it, as we reflect on the impossibility of even coming close to him, ought to discourage us and thus dampen our zeal to imitate him, may thus instead be very well suited to our passion for ideals that are more than human. /

But in order to be a good imitator, one must have some original- 58 ity; otherwise the imitation looks forced and unnatural—a bit off here and there, and out of keeping with everything else one does. True enough in all domains, this is especially so in the moral: virtue above all must be something experienced for oneself, practiced on one's own. Virtue which mechanically repeats what others do—virtue learned by rote—is clumsy and awkward, cannot stand firm as one gains experience and knowledge of the world, and turns out to have neither value nor merit. Hence countless uninteresting people, the mass of mankind who have no noble sentiments, no experience of difficult situations, no knowledge of circumstances in which one might display virtue, strength of character, or forbearance—people who aspire to resemble the original without even the remotest contact with similar situations and activities—have attempted to dignify their concerns by giving them the names of lofty virtues. This is why we have had such a multitude of plaintive sufferers who really have nothing wrong with them, so many persecuted individuals who are in fact free of oppression, or who indeed cannot rest content until they find persecutors, and such an abundance of people professing wisdom that nobody needs. The paradigm of virtue that men have fashioned in accordance with their ideal was naturally tinged with those virtues most conspicuously displayed in that ideal.* But the imitations have recurrently led to the degeneration and misapplication of these virtues. In this way the desire to instruct has bred dogmatism, and this in turn gave rise to intolerance.

The doctrine of divine providence, a concept indigenous to the

*This is why we have such great heroes in suffering, great teachers in martyrdom.

Christian religion, is a concept of reason, and is really not supposed to be applied to specific instances as such, since it is not a concept of [practical] understanding and therefore does not explain anything.[23]

Practical moral doctrines

A great many of those who generally oppose everything Christian have nonetheless shown the greatest respect for the morality of the Christian religion. For all the ridicule and other weapons they have loosed upon the doctrines of the Trinity, Atonement, and Original Sin, they have nonetheless become enchanted with the morality of Christendom and have extolled it as a great boon to the human race. Nowhere could the very purest moral system (morality that altogether excludes material principles) so unhesitatingly join forces with the Christian religion than precisely in the area of morality. And no matter how often still other opponents have found isolated remarks on the part of Jesus or his apostles, particular injunctions or expressions of opinion, to be / incompatible with a pure morality, it is no less certain that as a whole the spirit of Christ's moral teaching can be brought into harmony with the most sublime morality, that in fact it demands the most unqualified obedience to the moral law.

But the essential point is not whether the maxims of a pure morality are to be found in the teachings of Jesus; they are just as readily found in the writings of a Plato, a Xenophon, a Rousseau. Nor does it particularly matter if the practical principles have not been systematized, or even whether all duties and their respective motives have been specified. What does matter is in what light they are set forth, how they are bound together, and what the order of their importance is alleged to be.

John's message to the people was: Repent. Christ's: Repent and believe in the good tidings. The apostles': Believe in Christ. And it is the apostles' version that has held sway in all the schools, in the catechisms, and in sermons right up to the present. Even today, when the spirit, the ideas, of the time no longer reflect much need of repentance for wrongdoing, we are taught first (in order of impor-

23. In the German text this brief paragraph is actually an incomplete sentence. It is an important one, however, because its point, namely that "divine providence" is not an explanatory concept in the same way that those of the empirical sciences are meant to be, is not repeated elsewhere in these fragments.

tance if not time) to know Christ as the propitiator sacrificed to appease an outraged God for the sake of all mankind—each of whom
has need of expiation not just on occasion, but throughout his life,
indeed for the very fact that he exists. And although millions have
made similar sacrifice, giving their lives for lesser ends (their king,
their country, their beloved) and done so gladly, with a smile instead
of an anguished bloody sweat,* we are supposed to have such gratitude for this one person who suffered and died for us that his death
becomes the very centerpiece of our religion, the most solemn preoccupation of our imagination, and is supposed to lead us to reverence
for Christ and God. Our worship consists first of propagating his
name, and then, somewhere along the line, of piety, charity, etc. as
well. By detours of this sort we arrived at morality; we did not work
up to it, we just got around to it eventually. Thus while the reproach
that the Christian religion does not further morality at all would be
unjustified, it is evident that these moral detours—which are so readily taken for one's main (indeed only) objectives—have done much to
harm morality. The real end of morality had already been lost sight of
when salvation replaced it as the ultimate purpose of such teachings.

When faith is extolled the result is often complacent, lifeless acceptance—memorization, lip service, / idle sentiments—with no real   60
concern about good character or virtuous action. The way that the
apostles went about admitting people into their community had already changed radically from Christ's acceptance of those he regarded
as friends. The former were satisfied when a multitude of generally
ignorant people allowed themselves to be so bedazzled by an hour
or two of oratory that they believed the apostles' words outright and
let themselves be baptized; thus were they instantly made Christians
for life. Having been carried on for centuries, this manner of conversion is practiced in essentially the same way even today on the banks
of the Ganges, the Orinoco, and the St. Lawrence River.

The fact that our worshipful gratitude toward Christ and our popu-
larizing his name throughout the world is alleged to be our main
purpose and our primary duty, perfectly justifies the reproach made
by Sittah in *Nathan*.[24] For what is the point of sending missionaries

---

*One can well imagine how gladly they would have died for the human race.
24. Not his virtue; his name
    Is everywhere to be proclaimed . . .
                    Nathan, II, 1.

abroad when there are still immoral people among the Christians themselves? Not only the Catholics, but the Anglicans and the Protestants as well, have toiled, sweated, struggled, and even spent blood to set up costly missions in faraway places—all in order that a name and a legend might captivate the imagination of peoples who had already long ago fashioned a religion and gods appropriate to their needs.

[10]

[A. Introduction][25]

To write about the Christian religion is to risk being accused of erroneously portraying its aim and essence; and to go so far as to be critical toward some aspect of what one has portrayed is to invite the rejoinder that this is not really pertinent to Christianity but only to some caricature of it. And were one to insist on being shown a reliable systematization of pure Christianity, the scholars would answer in unison: "But haven't you read my compendium?" —But Gentlemen, the compendia you have written yourselves or on which you base your systems of belief are so at variance with one another that I have to ask you first to render them compatible before you declare that something is not part of the Christian religion. —Accordingly, in what follows here, anything considered as belonging to the Christian religion is either drawn directly out of the / New Testament or presently constitutes (with the exception of only a few textbooks and convictions espoused by a handful of enlightened individuals) a systematized version of the popular doctrine officially recognized by the Church Councils and their committees. In other words, it is still the line generally taken on the pulpit and in the schools, and is in any case the system by which the entire generation that has now come of age has been educated and instructed. This is why it is still important to shed light on various aspects of this whole scheme of salvation, at least until such a time as more salutary representations have won the day; by then such systems would be curiosities, of interest only to the investigator of the spirit of times gone by. Thus I hope

61

---

25. One of Hegel's marginal schemes runs: "A. Introduction. B. a) Doctrines; b) Traditions; c) Ceremonies; d) Public Religion." Cf. p. 94 below. In this draft, at any rate, Hegel seems never to have got past B. a.

that I have avoided the error of those who give others the itch in order to be able to scratch them. No reassurance would give me greater pleasure than learning that I did not need to call attention to all these modes of representation that strike me as scandalous, inasmuch as they have long since been forgotten—if only I could accept this assurance as being generally valid.

Religion's proper task is to strengthen, by means of the idea of God as moral lawgiver, what impels us to act ethically and to enhance the satisfaction we derive from performing what our practical reason demands, specifically with regard to the ultimate end that reason posits: the highest good. Because religion can do these things its purpose is compatible with that of civil legislators and administrators, who in turn can satisfy the natural human need for religion by promoting it through specific measures. But ordinarily the will of a nation has committed itself to a particular religion long before any government can institute it as a purpose of its own; and so all that is left for the government to do is protect it, propagate it, and keep it ever fresh in the public mind. —We all know, for instance, that in the many nations under monarchic rule one or another religion receives considerable support from the public establishment. Here the populace is rarely in a position to be able to investigate and choose for itself, and hence is disposed to receive instruction rather passively. Thus it is surely permissible to inquire whether a religion that must at one time have been appropriate for a people (otherwise they wouldn't have adopted it) is in this same form equally appropriate once circumstances have greatly changed. Was this religion so well-constituted, both as a universal and as a private religion, that it could maintain its dignity, appropriateness, and efficacy throughout all the changes in form of government and variations in level of enlightenment? Did the spirit of the people gradually discard or modify the dated aspects of their religion? Or wasn't it rather the case that those who were in power became also the effective / administrators of religion, it being in their 62 interest to keep a tight hold on the form of religion inherited from their ancestors and to pass this cherished treasure that had been entrusted to them on to their descendants? It has generally taken centuries before the need for changes has come to be recognized by a whole nation—and by then there is nothing that can delay them. Still, the people, usually satisfied to strike but once, have tended to let the initiative be wrested from them again, whereupon their very attachment to what has been newly won, coupled with their suspicion that this might be taken from them again, makes further progress and improvements impossible for centuries.

A religion can be considered with respect to
   a) its doctrines,
   b) its traditions,
   c) its ceremonies,
   d) its relation to the state, i.e. as a public, institutionalized religion.

What are the requisites of a folk religion with regard to these aspects? Do we find them present in the Christian religion?

[B. a) Doctrines]

(α) Man's practical reason poses for him the task of realizing, as the ultimate end of his striving, the highest good in the world, namely morality and a form of happiness commensurate with it.

I think I can safely assume that hope for eternal happiness (which is an almost universal doctrine of Christianity) is what interests the Christian most. To him everything else has merely a subordinate value; and God's good will is thus very important since he is the dispenser of this happiness. What his notion of happiness entails materially is to some extent compatible with what reason establishes. But while reason requires that one's basic way of thinking must be oriented to the moral law if one is to bring about the essential condition allowing for the highest good, the Christian religion is insistent upon belief in Christ and the power of his reconciliatory death as the essential condition of eternal happiness. Instead of this belief ultimately leading to morality (which would then be the true condition [of the good] and the belief merely a means), it constitutes, in and of itself, the whole basis for God's good will. Although they could never actually earn it, those who believe in Christ are granted eternal salvation by God's good will. /

63   This discrepancy regarding what ought to be mankind's highest law leads to a number of consequences, or rather rests on some noteworthy presuppositions: Try as he might, with all the honest zeal for the good he can muster, man, because of his utter incapacity for morality, can never reach the point of meriting true happiness. What

measure of it he does receive, he owes to the free and undeserved grace of God; from divine justice he would have nothing to expect but misery and punishment. Taken for granted here is that the good man incontestably deserves happiness, he may demand it as his right, he is worthy of it. The only trouble is that it has also been presupposed that to become a good man is impossible.

The list of examples that can be used to counter such notions is so long as to be tedious: Socrates, the many virtuous heathens, even whole tribes of innocent men. To which the wretched reply, so outrageous to a man of feeling who believes in virtue—hatched by some heartless father of the church and parroted ad nauseam by schoolboys no less shallow—has always been that these have merely displayed exemplary vices. The principle that the good person is worthy of happiness is deeply embedded in the universal moral nature of man. It is a principle that is generally expressed in the mode of a judgment of sound common sense, and is one which even the theologians presuppose in their doctrine of righteousness. But it is nonetheless a proposition that gives them trouble, one which they try to conceal, one which they are reluctant to acknowledge. For it is, after all, to some extent contrary to their fundamental principle regarding the expiatory suffering and death of Christ.

The tenet regarding the depravity not only of individual men but of human nature as such—one that experience contradicts wherever bad governments have not degraded mankind—would not have been put forth in such strength and detail if it were based merely on the feeble exegesis of a few scattered passages in scripture that seem to support it: it had to have been crucial to the whole [Christian enterprise]. One thought one could find in sacred scripture the physical cause of man's alleged depravity and antipathy toward the good. However repugnant reason must find this idea, it was carried to such an extent that even children were considered deserving of [divine] punishment. But if the will of man is really all that ineffectual (not to mention being allegedly susceptible to the influence of evil spirits), it ought rather to be declared free of all blame. For there can be no such thing as accountability where there is no practical freedom— where man is denied the capacity / to recognize the good as such, 64 to have respect for it, or to be able to prevail over his own sensuousness.—It was therefore entirely consistent that heathens were damned without mercy or compassion; and the philanthropic sentiment of those theologians who currently do not quite dare to give a straight-forward opinion on the subject stands in contradiction with the rest of their system.

So, inasmuch as man is incapable of it, morality cannot be made the foremost condition of salvation—otherwise there could be no salvation. Accordingly, the compassionate mercy of God provided a substitute for morality,[26] something of which man *is* capable, namely belief in Christ. However much one demands, as an indispensable component of faith, that it be activated in good works, it is not the latter, according to the dictum of the theologians, which primarily contains what would make us deserving, give us some inherent value, and elicit God's good will toward us. —But at this turn all that faith basically amounts to is persuading the understanding, or at least the imagination, that it should accept as true various things that to some extent are matters of mere historical credibility and to some extent are incompatible with the understanding.

Belief in the historical person of Christ is not based on any requirement of practical reason, but rests on the testimony of others. Reason tells us that, as far as it is concerned, what is of interest—what provides the ultimate purpose of man's being and activity, and serves as the keystone of the whole system in which one can find order, peace of mind, and a resolution of the most burdensome questions—has a purely rational principle and basis. A man needs to develop his rational capacity only in order to resolve such problems; and reason is quite accessible to anyone who is willing to hear its voice (one day [of reason] speaks to any other day). But historical belief is by its very nature limited: its dissemination is contingent upon circumstances, and it is a source not accessible to all. And yet it is alleged to be a necessary condition of God's being well-disposed toward us—a condition affecting our lot for all eternity. Now, we can pretend as modestly and humbly as we like to be ignorant of the ways and intentions of Providence (which in other areas we profess to have espied most exactly); we cannot really ask, for instance, why didn't nature give the animals human talents like our gifts of reason and morality. But even if, out of perverse arrogance (which could only be sustained by our presupposing that we are by nature depraved), / we are unwilling to place ourselves any higher on the

65

26. Hegel for some reason added, parenthetically: "(put in its place)".

ladder of being than countless [earlier] cultures, we would still have reason to expect that the means, the ways of educating ourselves to the kind of perfection which alone gives human beings a sense of worth—are available to the entire human race. —We are left with only two possible alternatives at this point. One is that the majority of the human race is excluded from the grace which, by virtue of our faith, pours down upon us, the chosen ones—we who by our own admission are at best as depraved as the rest of mankind and hence deserve nothing better. On this alternative we deprive our reason and our sense of human dignity of a crucial concept, namely that one is worthy of happiness on the basis of a moral life. We abolish the moral relationship of the deity to the world and mankind—the very concept of divine justice, by virtue of which alone his existence is of interest to us. And we deny that God's moral attributes are in any way knowable or determinable by us, that we can have any notion of his moral nature, of the way he judges people, or of what constitutes virtue in his eyes—despite our familiarity, through our Christian religion, with quite a number of utterly mysterious, transcendent attributes of God. —Our other alternative is to abandon all claim to such knowledge. We have to admit that this belief simply does not have the enormous importance that is claimed for it—that it is not the sole and exclusive condition on which human beings can comprehend something of their purpose on earth, on which they can have worth before God and reason.

The grounds for belief in [the life of] Christ rest on history. If due to the initial simplicity of its customs a people is still free of extensive class inequality, and if a historical event of this sort is played out on its soil, a tradition is passed on from parents to children which belongs to everyone in equal measure. However, once distinct classes begin to form in a nation, and the family elder is no longer at the same time the high priest, there will soon come into prominence a class of men serving as the trustees of traditions primarily through them. Such is especially the case when these traditions originate in a foreign land, amidst alien customs, and in a strange tongue; for then the original form of their ground and content is no longer possessed by everyone, and in order even to familiarize oneself with it, one has to put in a lot of time and master a complicated apparatus of pertinent information. But hereby the priestly class soon attains control over public belief—a power base which / can at the very least 66 perpetuate, and often greatly increase, its control in matters concerning the doctrines of the folk religion.

Believing* what is said by people we trust, or having faith in those that the state appoints in order to win our trust, is far easier than cultivating the habit of thinking for ourselves. And belief based on historical testimony, although it may occasionally prompt us to ask questions, does not naturally awaken the spirit of reflection. On the other hand, when moral or prudential principles are at issue, everyone feels called upon and entitled to weigh these with his own feelings and experiences and make some judgment as to their truth and applicability. But people are prone to believe the historical truths that they have been told from childhood on, to the point of not doubting them in the least; in this way they render themselves permanently incapable of examining their truth. Thus it is alleged that our salvation is based not on anything that our reason (our attentiveness to ourselves and to others, our reflectivity) could ever establish, but rather on the authority of those whom the state has specially entrusted with transmission of historical truths. Hence it is quite natural, one could say, that the employment and cultivation of the understanding, trust in one's own insights, and independence of conviction receive such meager encouragement from these authorities, and that such [virtues] are far from common.

For faith such as this, even though it may presume to distinguish itself from historically-based belief by virtue of a higher degree of vitality, a certain intensity of soul, there inevitably awaits a final reckoning. No matter how deeply it entrenches itself behind authority, no matter how artfully it seeks to ward off all counter-hypotheses and alternative possibilities by assembling a system that covers every conceivable circumstance (a system one cannot get at without becoming entangled in endless details), reason will still venture to subject it to critical scrutiny. And it will do so spontaneously, generating from within itself principles of possibility and plausibility irrespective of any such artificial historical structure predisposed to neglect reason and to claim primacy on historical grounds over the persuasiveness of rational truths.

Once reason has matured to the point of having a sense of autonomy, the conviction it has generated from within, and which is

---

*a matter of memory.

grounded inside itself, is so strong that it may find itself completely indifferent to such a historical faith and / its arguments; and for this it will be reproached with inexcusable rashness. Should faith be repeatedly dangled before reason's eyes in an attempt to subdue it before it has sufficient historical erudition to launch attacks of its own, reason may still stubbornly refuse to surrender and convert; for this it will be accused of willful blindness. On the other hand reason may try literally to destroy this historical belief by ridiculing it and pointing out the absurdity of its diverse accounts; it may treat sacred scripture as it would any other work of man, and allege that its texts may very well have been altered or that they are based only on folk beliefs, like the traditions of other peoples; it may even turn historical faith's own weapons against it, pointing out that what faith derives from the books that serve as its foundation cannot actually be found in those texts—that faith is forever tampering with their meaning ad hoc in order to accommodate them to itself. And for this, reason will be charged with lack of respect for the divine word, with malice and dishonesty.[27]

Faith in Christ is faith in a personified ideal (cf. pp. 88f above). ⟵

Why are human examples insufficient to fortify us in the struggle for virtue, to enable us to feel the divine spark in ourselves—the power which lies in us to achieve mastery over the sensuous? Why do we fail to realize that virtuous human beings are not merely flesh of our flesh, bone of our bone, but that they are also morally sensitive—are spirit of our spirit, power of our power? Alas, we have been persuaded that this capacity is alien to us, that man belongs only to the order of natural beings (and depraved ones at that). The idea of sanctity has been totally isolated and attached exclusively to a remote being; for it was assumed that this idea cannot be reconciled with that of containment within a sensuous nature. Thus although moral perfection could be attributed to this Being of Beings, its perfection would not constitute a part of our own essence, and its action in us would be possible only through some bond between it and ourselves, by its indwelling in us (*unio mystica*). This degrading view of human nature does not allow us to recognize ourselves in virtuous individuals; at this point the only ideal that could serve as a model of virtue would be a God-man. This might work if we could find something

27. This paragraph foreshadows Hegel's 1806 *Phenomenology*, Chapter VI, B. ⟵

truly divine in him—not his being the second person of the Godhead, begotten of the Father from all eternity, etc., but simply the
conformity of his whole character and spirit with the moral law. But
no matter how explicitly the letter of this law can be conveyed in
signs and words, it is ultimately / incumbent on us to elicit its [spirit
and] idea in ourselves.

68

  That the truly divine element in the idea of holiness was often
misunderstood and forgotten is shown by the disputes—often of the
life and death variety—between the scholars and the priests, i.e. among
the very individuals whose duty it was to maintain attentiveness to
the moral aspects of this idea. They quarreled over morally sterile
predicates like eternal generation, and argued about the exact way
in which the divine and human natures were united—the sort of pe-
ripheral concerns that are given exhaustive definition in learned tracts
and that end up being so subtle that they slip right through one's
fingers. Their differing opinions about these things have been made
into the essential concerns of religion. Such disputes not being confined to the study, the people and their governments have been summoned to use force against all parties who think differently, allowing
these to repent of their errors only in blood or in the dungeon. Thus,
obviously, what is essential to an ideal was overlooked or miscon-
strued—namely that it be ideal, that it be divine in our eyes. But
other equally dismaying developments make it no less clear that this
was not the only way in which people could misunderstand the ideal
and begin clinging to quite secondary aspects of it—sacrificing their
own blood along with everybody else's for a mere name, for slogans
associated with the ideal, for words alleged to originate with it (cf.
pp. 90 and 91 above).

  By what arrangements could it be brought to pass that in Christ
not just a human being, not merely his name, but virtue itself be
known and loved? The answer to this question depends upon the
solution to the problem of how a people's receptivity to morality and
moral ideas can be cultivated—a solution whose consideration would
run far beyond our purview. Our object here is merely the interest
which the Christian religion, quite incidentally, wishes to take in
cultivating such receptivity by means of the circuitous paths of its faith.

  As matters stand, the axis around which the entire hope of our
salvation turns is belief in Christ as mediator between God and the
world. He is the one who bore in our stead the punishments which

the human species had deserved—in part because of a depravity inherent in its nature, in part because it had incurred them through deeds of its own. These sufferings of a guiltless one—for he was God—are supposed somehow to subtract from the boundless guilt of the human species and reckon up in our favor. In comparison with this ground floor of the edifice of Christian belief, the other doctrines are to be embraced merely as so many buttresses. And this is why it was so necessary to insist / on the worthlessness of mankind and on its inability ever to attain any worth in a natural way. Hence the doctrine of Christ's divinity: for only the suffering of such a one could counterbalance the guilt of the whole human species. Hence also the doctrine of God's free grace, since the event to which our salvation is bound would remain unknown to half the world through no fault of its own. And hence, too, the development of a number of other doctrines similarly connected with the central one. / 69

[11]²⁸

Today those masses of humanity who no longer possess public virtue and have been contemptuously relegated to an oppressed condition need other props, other modes of solace that compensate them for their wretchedness without further jeopardizing their self-esteem. The inner certainty that stems from faith in God and immortality has to be replaced with external assurances, by belief in people who are adept at creating the impression that they are better informed regarding matters of faith. —By contrast, the free republican, in keeping with the spirit of his people, devoted his energies—indeed his very life—to his fatherland; and he did so out of duty, without placing such value on his own efforts that he could presume to expect compensation or reimbursement. He toiled on behalf of his idea, his duty: what could he ever claim in return? All he expected for his honest efforts was to join the company of heroes in the Elysian Fields or in Valhalla, and to be more happy there than here only in that he would be free of the troubles of frail mankind. —So, too, when someone has taken it upon himself, as a maxim of reason, to obey 70

---

28. There is a consensus among Nohl, Schüler, and Harris that this fragment is also from 1794.

nature and necessity, honoring this law as sacred no matter how incomprehensible we may find it to be, what claims to compensation
are left to him? What indemnification can an Oedipus claim for his
undeserved sufferings, inasmuch as he believed himself to be an agent
of fate acting under the sway of fate? — On the other hand, only
a people of the utmost depravity, of the profoundest moral impotence, is capable of adopting as its maxim blind submission to the
evil whims of infamous men. Only a protracted state of misery culminating in utter obliviousness of anything better for man could bring
a people to such a pass. But then, having been abandoned by itself
as much as by the gods, it sees only to its own private affairs, and
has to be reassured by signs, miracles, etc. from the deity that a life
in the future is still possible for it; for it can no longer muster this
faith from within. But at this point there is no longer any prospect
of comprehending the idea of morality and building one's faith on
it (such ideas have lost their vitality and are now mere chimeras);
71   one can only / latch one's faith onto some individual, lean on someone who can serve as an example, an object of admiration. Hence
the warm and open reception of the Christian religion once the Romans had lost their public virtue and their empire was in decline.
Hence, too, humanity's recovery of its capacity for ideas once its
centuries-long preoccupation with the individual in his particularity
had waned, i.e. once the very thing that makes any individual truly
interesting began to blossom in all its splendor, namely his existence
as an idea sustained in our own thought and thus proper to our own
nature (the doctrine of man's depravity having lost its hold on us,
despite our continuing experience of human corruption) — that is to
say, once we had begun to appreciate all that is fine in human nature
(instead of transferring it onto an alien individual, retaining for ourselves nothing but the loathsomeness of which our nature is capable)
and joyfully to recognize and claim it as our own work, thereby re-
gaining a sense of self-respect instead of, as before, regarding everything specific to us as contemptible.

When we have only a private existence, our highest interest has
to be our love of [our own individual] life, of its comforts and adorn-
ments; our morality is then constituted by a system of prudence. But
now that moral ideas can play a role in the lives of human beings,
such blessings sink in value; constitutions that merely guarantee life
and property are no longer regarded as the best. And the whole timo-

rous contrivance [of religion], this artificial system of drives and means of consolation in which so many thousands of weak souls have found comfort, is becoming more and more superfluous. Hence now the system of religious truth, which heretofore has always taken on the color of the time and its political constitutions — reckoning humility, i.e. consciousness of impotence, to be the highest virtue and looking to sources outside ourselves for everything (including to some extent evil itself) — can begin to attain a true and independent worth of its own.

The Life of Jesus[1]

(1795)

Pure reason, transcending all limits, is divinity itself—whereby and in accordance with which the very plan of the world is ordered (John 1). Through reason man learns of his destiny, the unconditional purpose of his life. And although at times reason is obscured, it continues to glimmer faintly even in the darkest age, for it is never totally extinguished.

Among the Jews John[2] reawakened the people to this, their own dignity—not as to something alien, but rather as to something they should be able to find within, in their true self. They were not to seek it in their lineage, nor in the desire for happiness, nor by devoting themselves to some dignitary, but rather in the cultivation of the spark of divinity allotted them—their proof of descendance, in a higher sense, from the Godhead itself. The cultivation of reason is the sole source of truth and tranquility; and John, never pretending to possess reason exclusively or as something rare, insisted that all men could uncover it in themselves.—But even more credit is due to Christ: for his reformation of man's corrupt principles of conduct, for his recognition of genuine morality, and for his purer worship of God.

In the Judaean village (Matt. 1:2) called Bethlehem Jesus was born to Mary and to Joseph,* who could trace his lineage (it being Jewish custom to put stock in family trees) back to David. In keeping /
76 with Jewish law Jesus was circumcised a week after his birth (Luke 2:21ff.); but nothing is known of his upbringing except that he manifested an exceptional and precocious intellect (Luke 2:41), and was very much interested in religious matters. One incident occurring in his twelfth year exemplifies this: having gone off from his parents and caused them considerable worry, he was found in the temple of Jerusalem among the priests, whom he had astonished with

1. According to Hegel's own entries at the beginning and end of his manuscript, this essay was written between May 9 and July 24, 1795.

2. John the Baptist.

*They were in fact residents of Nazareth in Galilee, but had to journey to Bethlehem, Joseph's family seat, in order to be enrolled in the census of the Jewish population then being conducted on the orders of Augustus.

his insights and, for his age, unusual powers of reasoning. But aside from this the only information that has come down to us concerning his early upbringing and the remarkable development that took place in him up to the age of thirty, when he appeared publicly as an educated man and teacher (Luke 3; Matt. 3), is that he came to know John who called himself "the baptist" (it being his custom to immerse those who responded to his appeal for reform).

John felt that he was called upon to awaken his countrymen to purposes higher than mere pleasure, to expectations better than the restoration of the former splendor of the Jewish nation. Characteristically, he dwelt and taught in remote areas, and satisfied his needs in the simplest way—he clothed himself in a camel-hair coat and leather belt, and fed himself on the honey of wild bees and the edible locusts of the region. Concerning his teaching only this is known: he called the people to change the very meaning of their lives and to manifest this transformation by their deeds. Whenever confronted by Jews claiming that, as descendants of Abraham, they had no need to do anything like this in order to win divine favor, John simply told them they were wrong; but when someone remorseful over his past conduct approached, he would baptize him, symbolizing that hereby the stain of corruption was being removed much as one washes away impurities.

Upon coming to John, Jesus too was baptized. But when John detected in him the great capacities he was later to manifest, he insisted that Jesus had no need of baptism; and since he considered it no honor to have disciples, persons closely tied to him, he urged many to turn to Jesus for instruction. And later he even expressed great joy (John 3:27ff.) upon hearing of the many listeners Jesus was finding and (although Jesus himself did not baptize) of the multitude being baptized by his friends.

In the end (Matt. 14) John fell victim to the injured vanity of a woman / and of Herod, the local sovereign. Having reproached Herod for his intimacy with Herodias (Herod's own sister-in-law), John was thrown into jail; but he wasn't done away with—Herod didn't dare go that far, since the populace regarded him a prophet. However, at one of Herod's lavish birthday feasts Herodias' daughter[3] put on such a display of talent as a dancer and so charmed Herod that he called upon her to make some request of him—a favor he would grant even

77

3. Salome.

if it be for half his kingdom. At this point the mother, previously having had to hold back the desire for revenge ignited by her insulted pride, prevailed upon her daughter to request that John be killed. Herod, lacking the good sense to realize or the courage to attest in front of his guests that the word he had given did not extend as far as a criminal act, had the head of John delivered to the child on a platter furnished by her mother. His body was buried by his disciples.

Aside from the above we have very few indications as to how Jesus developed spiritually during this period of his life. But once, during an hour of solitary reflection (Luke 4; Matt. 4), it occurred to him that perhaps by studying nature he might, in league with higher spirits, actually seek to transform base matter into a more precious substance, into something more immediately useful to man, e.g. converting stones into bread. Or perhaps that he might establish his own independence of nature altogether while hurtling down from a high place. But as he reflected on the limits nature has placed on man's power over her, he rejected such notions, realizing that it is beneath man's dignity to strive for this sort of power when he already has within himself a sublime power transcending nature altogether, one whose cultivation and enhancement is his true life's calling.

On another occasion there ran before his mind's eye all the things that man counts as great and worthy objects of his activity—to rule over millions, to be on the lips of half the world, to see thousands dependent on one's will and whim, or to live happily in pursuit of pleasure and the gratification of whatever one wishes, having everything that rouses one's vanity or stimulates one's senses. But reflecting further on the conditions under which one could attain these, even supposing one intended to make use of them only for the well-being of mankind—realizing that he would have to subject himself /
78 to his own and others' passions, forget his higher worth and relinquish his self-respect—he rejected the notion of bringing such wishes to fruition and gave no further thought to the matter. Determined to remain forever true to what was indelibly written in his heart, i.e. the eternal law of morality, he revered only him whose sacred will can be swayed by nothing but this law.

Only in his thirtieth year did he appear in public as a teacher. His first discourses were confined to a few individuals, but he was soon joined by a group of friends who, either because they liked what he taught or were attracted by his growing acclaim, accompanied him virtually everywhere (John 1:35–51). Through teaching and example he sought to rid this group of the narrow spirit of Jewish prejudice and national pride and fill them instead with his own spirit, which found merit only in a virtue that was not tied to a particular nation or to particular institutions.

Now although he spent most of his time in Galilee, specifically in Capernaum, he would usually travel to Jerusalem for the Jewish high feasts, particularly for the annual Passover. The first time he came to Jerusalem (John 2:13ff.) after his public emergence as a teacher, he was involved in a shocking incident and made quite a stir. As he entered the temple, where all the inhabitants of Judaea would gather in communal prayer, raising themselves above the petty concerns of everyday life as they approached the Deity, Jesus encountered a crowd of merchants speculating on the religiosity of the Jews, selling them all sorts of goods to be used for sacrifice, and indeed taking special advantage, right there in the temple, of the influx of people from all over Judaea gathering for the feasts. Outraged by this blatant commercialism, Jesus drove the whole crowd of hucksters out of the temple.

He found that his teaching had an effect on many people; but since he was keenly aware of the Jews' attachment to deep-rooted national prejudices and their lack of a sense for anything higher than this, he did not seek closer dealings with them or place much confidence in their conviction. On the whole he did not deem them capable of such, did not believe them to be cut from a cloth from which something greater could be fashioned. As for himself, he was too far removed from vanity to feel in the least honored by the acclaim of a crowd of people, and was not weak enough to draw any more support from such acclaim / than his own conviction already provided. 79 He needed no plaudits, no external authority to believe in reason.

But the attention Jesus had so far attracted (John 3) made little apparent impression on the priests and educators of the people, or at least they pretended to look upon him only with contempt. Yet one of them, Nicodemus, felt motivated to become more closely acquainted with Jesus in order to determine whether there was anything new and different, or indeed anything worthwhile, in his teaching. He came in the darkness of night, lest he expose himself to ridicule or hatred, and said to Jesus: "I've come to you for instruction. Everything I've heard about you convinces me that you are an emissary of God sent from heaven, and that God dwells in you." Jesus replied, "Yes. And indeed anyone who does not have his origin in heaven, who does not have divine power within him, is no citizen of the kingdom of God." "But how," Nicodemus retorted, "is a man to relinquish his natural condition? He would have to return to his mother's womb and be born as someone else—as a being of another kind." "Man as man," Jesus answered, "is not an altogether sensuous being; he is not by nature just confined to pleasure-seeking impulses. He has spirit in him too; as a rational being he has received as his inheritance a spark of the divine essence. Just as you undeniably hear the howling of the wind and can feel it blow, though you can neither control it nor even know whence it comes and whither it goes, so this autonomous and immutable power makes its presence known to you from within. But just how this power is linked with the rest, with our changeable human sensibility, and how it can gain ascendancy over our sensuous capacity—this we do not know."

Nicodemus confessed that these were ideas with which he was unfamiliar, and Jesus exclaimed, "What! You are a teacher in Israel and you don't grasp what I am saying? Let me assure you that my conviction in this matter is every bit as alive as the certainty I have concerning what I see and hear. But then how can I expect you to believe it on my word when you don't even hear the inner testimony of your own spirit, of the divine voice? Only this voice from heaven can instruct you concerning the higher demands of reason; and only by 80 believing in it and heeding it / does one find peace of mind and true greatness, and thus discover the dignity of which mankind is capable. Indeed, by endowing man with reason the Deity so distinguished humankind from the rest of nature that man came alive with the reflected splendor of the divine essence; and only through his faith in reason does man fulfill this high destiny. Reason does not condemn the natural impulses, but governs and refines them; and whoever does not listen to it—by not duly appreciating its light, by failing to nourish it in himself—passes judgment on himself, having thus shown by his actions what sort of a fellow he is. Such a man shrinks away from reason's light, for it imposes morality as a matter of duty; his evil works, which would otherwise fill him with shame, self-contempt, and remorse, bristle at its illumination. But whoever undertakes his tasks with self-honesty approaches reason's tribunal willingly, fearing neither its reprimands nor the self-knowledge it gives him; he does not need to conceal his actions, since they but attest to the spirit which animates him, the spirit of the rational world, the spirit of divinity."

Jesus left Jerusalem (John 4) when he heard that the sheer number of those applauding his teaching was drawing the attention of the Pharisees. Journeying back to Galilee by the road through Samaria, he sent his disciples ahead into the city to buy food, while he stopped at a well which had allegedly been owned by Jacob, one of the fathers of the Jewish people. Here he met a Samaritan woman, whom he asked to fetch him up a drink of water. She expressed surprise that he, a Jew, would request a drink from a Samaritan — their two nations having such an intense religious and political hatred of one another that there was absolutely no intercourse between them. Jesus answered her: "If you were acquainted with my principles, you would not have judged me as being just another Jew. You wouldn't have had misgivings about requesting the same of me. And I would have made you aware of another well, one with living water. Whoever drinks from it has his thirst quenched once and for all; and its water flows in a stream leading to eternal life." "I hear that you are a wise man," replied the Samaritan woman. "And I wish you would clear up this disagreement that divides our religion from yours: our elders perform their divine service here on Mount Garizim, whereas you maintain that Jerusalem alone is the place where one should worship the Almighty." "Believe me, woman," Jesus answered, "a time is coming when you will no longer celebrate any divine service, / whether on 81 Garizim or in Jerusalem — a time when nobody will any longer suppose that divine service is limited to prescribed rituals or to a specific place. The time will come — indeed it is already upon us — when those who truly revere their God will worship the universal father in the true spirit of religion. These alone are pleasing to him; their worship of God is authentic, being animated solely by the spirit of reason and its flower, the moral law."

The report which the woman gave about Jesus and her conversation with him led her townspeople to form a very high opinion of him, inducing many Samaritans to seek him out in order to learn from him. While Jesus talked with them, his disciples returned, urging him to eat. But he responded: "Never mind that for now. I am not all that preoccupied with bodily nourishment; my concern is to do the will of God and carry out the task of improving mankind. Your thoughts are fixed on food and the coming harvest. Widen your perspective. Look around you at the harvest that is ripening for humankind: this seed is maturing too, even though you have not sown these fields. Here and there the germ of goodness which nature implanted in the hearts of men has developed spontaneously; and it is your task to tend to these delicate blossoms, to look after them, to continue the work that nature has begun, and to bring the seed to maturity." At the request of the Samaritans, Jesus remained with them for two days and gave them the opportunity to confirm firsthand the high opinion they had formed of him through the woman's account.

After two days Jesus resumed his journey to Galilee (John 4:43; Matt. 4:12ff; Luke 4:14), and at every stopping place he summoned the people to change their dispositions and improve their ways (Matt. 4:17). He sought to awaken them from their slumber, from their barren and idle hope that a Messiah would soon appear to restore the splendor of Jewish public worship and the magnificence of the Jewish state. "Do not wait for someone else," he implored them; "you must undertake your own improvement. Set yourselves a higher aim than to become once again what the Jews of old were. Better yourselves — then will you bring forth the Kingdom of God." Thus did Jesus teach everywhere: in Capernaum and on Lake Genezareth, both publicly and in places reserved for instruction. And on one occasion at his birthplace, Nazareth, while he was explaining to the people a passage
82 from their sacred books, they asked themselves "But / isn't this just Joseph's son, who was born and raised among us?" Indeed the Jewish prejudice to the effect that the one they awaited as their savior had to be of noble descent and make his appearance in pomp and splendor was insuperable; so eventually his fellow townsmen drove him from the city, prompting him to cite the adage that nowhere does a prophet count for less than in his native land.

It was at about this point that he encountered (Matt. 4:18–22. c. 1. parall.) Peter and Andrew, along with James and John, all busily engaged in their work as fishermen. He asked them to come with him, saying to Peter: "Let the fish be; I will make you into a fisher of men."

By this period of his life (Matt. 4:25) the number of his supporters had become considerable, with people from many cities and villages coming out to accompany him. At one such numerous gathering he spoke roughly as follows:

"Fortunate (Matt. 5) are the humble and the poor; the heavenly realm is their lot.

"Fortunate, too, are those who endure suffering; one day they shall find solace.

"Fortunate are those inclined to gentleness; they shall know the joys of peace.

"And fortunate are those who thirst for justice; their yearning shall be fulfilled.

"Fortunate are those who feel compassion; for them too there will be compassion.

"Blessed are the pure of heart; for them holiness is very near.

"Happy are those who love peace—you will be called God's children.

"And blessed are those who are persecuted in the quest for integrity, enduring defamation and disgrace for it—be glad and rejoice, for you are the citizens of a divine realm.

"Of you, my friends, I would like to be able to say that you are the salt of the earth. But if salt loses its savor and blends indistinguishably with everything else, what are we to season with? So too, if the power of goodness were to die in you, your deeds would perish right along with the rest of mankind's pointless preoccupations. Be as lights to the world, showing yourselves in such way that your deeds illuminate all men and enkindle the better impulses within them, that they might learn to look upward to higher purposes and to our father in heaven.

"Do not believe for an instant that I have come to declare that the laws are no longer valid. I have not come to annul what the laws demand, but rather to make them complete, to breathe spirit into these lifeless / bones. Heaven and earth may pass away, but not the demands of the moral law nor the obligation to obey them. Whoever absolves himself from adherence to them is unworthy to be called a citizen of God's realm, while he who not only complies with them himself but teaches others to honor them will be highly esteemed in the heavenly realm. The one basic condition that I add, in order to make the entire system of laws complete, is this: You must not remain satisfied, like the scribes and Pharisees among you, with observing the mere letter of the law; although human tribunals may have this alone as their object, you must act out of respect for duty and in the spirit of the law.

"Let me give you an example from your legal code. You are all familiar with the ancient commandment 'Thou shalt not kill; whoever kills is to be hauled before the tribunal.' I say that it isn't just the fact of someone's death that constitutes a crime deserving punish-

83

ment. When anyone is unjustifiably angry toward his brother — although no earthly court could punish him for it — he is, in keeping with the law's spirit, no less deserving of punishment than a killer.

"In like manner, you are commanded to offer sacrifices at specified times. But if, as you approach the altar, you remember that you have offended someone and that he is still disturbed over it, then let your offering sit before the altar and go to your brother, extending your hand in atonement, for only then will you have approached the altar in a manner pleasing to God.

"Another of your commandments says 'Thou shalt not commit adultery.' But I say to you that not only is the actual deed a transgression, the very lust itself is sure sign of the heart's impurity. It does not matter what the propensity is — nor how natural or close to your heart it is. Resist it. If necessary, do injury to it. But do not let it drag you into deviating from what is right, and thus gradually undermine and destroy your principles. And do this even if the gratification of your impulses does not violate the letter of the law.

"Another ancient law is 'Do not take an oath falsely.' But if you have true regard for yourselves then any assurance, any promise indicated by even so much as a mere Yes or No, ought to be just as sincere, just as sacred and inviolable as an oath in the presence of the Deity. For your Yes or No must only be given if you fully intend to act accordingly before all eternity.

"Consider as well the civil law 'An eye for an eye, a tooth for a tooth.' Do not let this juridical precept govern your private life either in response to an insult or when acknowledging a kindness. Give up vengefulness in favor of the nobler sentiments / of gentleness and goodness, and, indifferent to the possession of property, do not insist upon your own advantage however often it may seem justified.

"You have also been told to love your friends and country, although you may hate your enemies and foreigners. But I say, if you cannot love your enemies, at least respect the humanity in them. For those who curse you, wish that good come to them; for those who hate you, do good to them. For those who lie about you to others, seeking to use them to make you miserable, intercede on their behalf. In this way you become true children of the father in heaven, alike in spirit to the All-bountiful himself, who lets his sun shine upon both good and bad, who lets the rain fall equally on the just and the unjust. For if you love only those who love you, do good only to those who do good to you, or lend only in order to receive an equivalent value in return (Luke 6:35), what have you accomplished? All this is a matter of natural feeling, which even the wicked would not dispute. Toward your duty you would have as yet done nothing. To be holy is your goal, in the same way as the Deity is holy.

"Liberality and the giving of alms (Matt. 6) are commendable virtues; but like the foregoing commandments, if they are put into practice not in the spirit of virtue but merely for show, then they are entirely without merit. So if you want to give alms, don't spread news of your deed or have it circulated as do hypocrites who hope to be praised to the skies. Do it so privately that the left hand does not know what the right hand is giving. Your reward (if you have need of the notion of a reward as incentive) is the quiet thought of having done well. For although the world may little know the author of your action, even what you do on a small scale—like the aid you tender in misfortune and the comfort you offer the sick—has an effect whose bounty is eternally rich.

"When you pray, do not be like the hypocrite—going down on your knees in the temple, folding your hands in the street, burdening your neighbors with your singing—all in order to be noticed. The prayers of hypocrites bear no fruit; but yours, whether within your chamber or without, should raise your spirit above the petty goals people set for themselves, and above the appetites which drive them to and fro. The thought of the holy should remind you of the law engraved in your bosoms and fill you with a respect for it that cannot be compromised by any of the lures of the inclinations. And do not suppose that the essence of prayer consists in a lot of / words; people 85 imagine that by means of these they can curry favor with God and be able to learn something about him and about the design of his eternal wisdom. Do not be like them in this. Your father knows what you need even before you ask him for it. Thus natural needs, wants, and inclinations cannot be the proper object of your prayer; for how can you know whether the gratification of these is the true purpose of the Holy One's design? The spirit of your prayer should be such that, animated by the idea of what is divine, your firmly resolve, before God, to dedicate your entire life to virtue.

"This prayerful spirit might be articulated something like this: 'Father of mankind, to whom all of heaven is subject, you, who alone are all holy, be for us the image* that we strive to approximate, so that some day your kingdom will come, a kingdom in which all rational beings will make nothing but the law their rule of conduct. To this idea all inclinations, even the cry of nature itself, will eventually be subjected. Conscious of our imperfections in face of your holy will, how could we set ourselves up as stern or indeed even vengeful judges of our brothers? We mean to work on ourselves instead, to improve our hearts, to purify that which moves us to act, and gradually to purge our dispositions of evil so as to become more like you, whose holiness and bliss are alone unending.'

"A sure sign of growth in moral perfection is the increase of brotherly love in you and your readiness to forgive—not the accumulation of worldly treasures, which you can never call entirely your own. Gold and silver, beauty, dexterity, and the rest all come and go; such things change with the tide—they rust away, they are devoured by insects, they are stolen; but none of them fills your soul anyway. Gather instead an imperishable treasure within yourselves, a moral wealth; only a treasure of this sort can you call your own in the full sense of the word, for it attaches to your deepest self. The forces of nature, the evil wills of men, even death have no power over it. The eye serves as the body's lamp; when sound it guides the body in all it does, but when defective it leaves the body awkward in everything. So too, if the light of the soul, the light of reason, grows dim, how are any of our drives and inclinations supposed to obtain their true bearing? Furthermore, just as one cannot serve two masters with equal fervor, so likewise is the service of God and reason incompatible with / devotion to the senses. The one excludes the other—or else there ensues a wretched and pathetic vacillation between them.

"This is why I exhort you to tear yourselves away from your endless preoccupation with what to eat, what to drink, and how to dress; for most people such needs describe the whole orbit of their endeavors and, judging by the importance they place on them, appear to constitute their very destiny, the be-all and end-all of their existence. Is there truly to be found no higher need in the human soul than that of nourishment and clothing? Look at the carefree birds in the sky: they do not sow, they do not reap, they do not heap up things in barns; the father of nature has provided for their nourishment.

*ideal

Isn't your destiny higher than theirs? Could you really be condemned by nature to exert all the noble powers of your soul in the gratification of the stomach's needs? You expend so much effort on adorning and beautifying the form which nature gave you; but can your vanity, with all its expenditure of wit and anxious concern, add one inch to your height? Or look at the flowers in the fields, which bloom so gloriously today only to be turned into hay tomorrow; could Solomon in all his splendor have rivaled such natural beauty? Therefore rid yourselves of some of this anguished obsession with how to feed and clothe yourselves. The highest goal of your endeavors should be the Kingdom of God, and the morality by means of which alone you may become worthy of being its citizens. Then the rest will take care of itself.

"Do not be harsh in your judgments of others (Matt. 7); for the very standard you use will redound on you, and this may not always turn out to your advantage. Why is it that you are so fond of seeing the smaller mote in the eye of the other, and fail to notice the much larger one in your own? Hypocrites! First remove your own, then give thought to treating someone else's. Reform yourselves first, before you would undertake to reform others. How can the blind show the blind the way—won't both fall into the ditch? Or can the teacher make the pupil more capable than he himself is? (Luke 6:40) And when you do want to better the lot of others, do not turn to just anyone imprudently and indiscriminately. Do not throw the sacred (ring) to the dogs, or pearls to swine: they would only trample it under as they turned to devour you. / Approach people imploringly   87
and often they will yield to you. Seek out a side from which they can be reached; you will find one. Knock softly and you will be admitted.

"To act only on principles that you can will to become universal laws among men, laws no less binding on you than on them"* —this

---

*The general rule of prudence is: Do unto others as you would have others do unto you (the rule of conventional morality). [Editor's note: It would seem that Kant's footnote in the *Grundlegung* of 1785, in which he explains the unfitness of the Golden Rule as a genuine moral principle, did not escape Hegel's attention. Kant had written: "Let it not be thought that the banal '*quod tibi non vis fieri, etc.*' could here serve as guide or principle, for it is only derived from the principle and is restricted by various limitations. It cannot be a universal law, because it contains the ground neither of duties to one's self nor of the benevolent duties to others (for is the fundamental law of morality, the sum and substance of all moral legislation and the sacred books of all peoples. Enter the temple of virtue through this gate of righteousness. It is narrow, to be sure; the path to it is perilous and your companions will be few. Far more sought-after is the palace of corruption and depravity, whose gateway is wide and whose streets are smooth. Along the way, be particularly on guard against false teachers who approach you with the gentle demeanor of a lamb, beneath which they hide the cravings of a ravenous wolf. You have a reliable sign by which to unmask their hypocrisy: judge them in accordance with their works. Surely one does not gather grapes from thorn bushes or figs from thistles. All good trees bear good fruit, and all bad ones bad fruit; one that bears bad fruit is not good, just as one that bears good fruit is not diseased (Luke 6:43).

"By their fruits, then, you shall know them. Goodness springs forth from the wealth of a good heart, evil from what fills a bad heart (Luke 6:45). So do not let yourselves be deceived by mere pious words; not everyone who cries out to God, who offers him prayers and sacrifice, is a member of his kingdom, but only he who does God's will, which is disclosed to man in the law of his own reason. In eternity, before the judge of the world, there will be many who will say: 'Lord, Lord, when we performed wondrous deeds, exorcising evil spirits and doing other great things, did we not invoke your name, did we not praise and thank you for them as though they were your work?' They will be answered: 'What was the point of your miracles, your prophecies, and your other grand accomplishments? Was this what life was all about? God does not recognize you as his. You miracle-makers, you soothsayers, you performers of great deeds— you are not citizens of his realm. Your actions were evil; morality alone is the criterion of what is pleasing to God.'

"Those who have heard these principles and have internalized them I compare with a wise man who has built his house on solid rock. When a storm comes and floods roar all about, when the winds blow,

---

many a man would gladly consent that others should not benefit him, provided only that he might be excused from showing benevolence to them). Nor does it contain the ground of obligatory duties to another, for the criminal would argue on this ground against the judge who sentences him. And so on." —Immanuel Kant, *Foundations of the Metaphysics of Morals,* tr. L. W. Beck. Bobbs-Merrill, 1959, p. 48n.]

they beat upon his house as upon everybody else's. But it does not
fall, for it has been erected on / rock. —Those who, even though
they have heard this teaching, do not act on it I compare with a fool
who has built his house on sand. When the storm comes and hits
his house with its weak foundation, it collapses with a crash."

This speech made a great impression on his hearers, for he spoke
with force and vigor, and his subject was such as is of the highest
concern to mankind.

From this time on, the crowds seeking to hear Jesus (Matt. 9; Mark
2:13) grew even larger. But the attention being paid him by the Pharisees
and the Jewish priesthood was increasing as well. To escape both the
clamor of the former and the snares of the latter, he frequently re-
treated into solitude. During one sojourn in Galilee he passed a customs-
house and saw an official named Matthew* sitting there [at work],
whom he invited to accompany him, and later on deemed worthy
of joining his more intimate circle. Then he dined with him along
with other publicans. Since among the Jews 'publican' and 'sinner'
were synonymous terms, the Pharisees expressed their astonishment
over this to Jesus' friends. But when Jesus heard this, he said to them:
"The healthy have no need of a doctor, only the ill. But as you go
about your business, reflect on the meaning of what (Hos. 6) is written somewhere in your sacred books: 'Not sacrifices but uprightness
are pleasing to me.'"

Eventually it occurred to some of the disciples of John the Baptist
that while they and the Pharisees fasted often, the friends of Jesus
did not. When he was questioned about this, Jesus answered: "What
would cause them to have genuine sorrow? The time will surely come
when their teacher will be taken from them too, just like yours will
be torn from you. Then they will have reason to fast! But should
I demand an austere way of life at all? It would not be in keeping
either with what they are used to or with my principles, which all
the less permit me to impose observation of specific practices on others."

Since another Passover was approaching (John 5), Jesus went to
Jerusalem. During his stay there, the Jews were greatly offended that
on one occasion he performed an act of kindness for a poor and sick
person on the Sabbath. They regarded this as a desecration of their

*In all probability this is the same story and the same person dealt with in Luke
5:27 and Mark 2:14, where the man appears under the name of Levi.

89   holy / day, and thought that Jesus was presumptuously exempting himself from a God-given commandment, indeed usurping a right belonging only to God and equating his own authority with that of the Deity. Jesus told them: "When you regard your ecclesiastical statutes and positive precepts as the highest law given to mankind, you fail to recognize man's dignity and his capacity to derive from his own self the concept of divinity and the comprehension of the divine will. Whoever does not honor this capacity within himself does not revere the Deity. That which a human being is able to call his self, that which transcends death and destruction and will determine its own just deserts, is capable of governing itself. It makes itself known as reason; when it legislates, it does not depend on anything beyond itself; nor can it delegate a different standard of judgment to any other authority in heaven or on earth.

"I do not pass off what I teach as some notion of my own, as something that belongs to me. I do not demand that anyone should accept it on my authority, for I am not seeking glory. I submit it only to the judgment of universal reason, that it might determine each individual to belief or nonbelief. But how could you allow reason to count as the highest criterion of knowledge and belief, since you have never heard the divine voice, have never heeded the resonance of this voice in your hearts, and so now refuse to pay attention to someone who strikes this chord? For you fancy yourselves to be in exclusive possession of the knowledge of God's will, and make what is allegedly due to you in preference to all other human beings the special object of your ambition. You keep appealing to Moses, always to Moses, and so base your faith upon the alien authority of a single individual! Simply read your own holy books—supposing you have the spirit of truth and virtue—and you will find evidence of this spirit there. And you will also find an indictment of the pride with which you flatter yourselves; indeed your narrowness does not allow you to lift your eyes to anything loftier than soulless erudition and mechanical customs."

Several other incidents (Matt. 12:1–8; Luke 6:1–5) gave the Pharisees occasion to reproach Christ and his disciples for desecrating the Sabbath. One day he was walking through a corn field with his friends. They were hungry, and tore off some ears and ate the kernels (or it may have been a species of oriental beans)—something which at other times was entirely permissible. Some Pharisees who saw this called /

Christ's attention to the fact that his disciples were acting in viola- 90
tion of the Sabbath. But Christ answered them: "Don't you remember the history of your people? David, when he was hungry, ate the
consecrated bread from the temple and moreover distributed it among
his companions. [Have you forgotten] that the priests in the temple
perform a variety of functions on the Sabbath as well? Is the temple
supposed to sanctify these functions? I say that a human being is more
than a temple—that a person, not a particular place, hallows actions
or makes them unholy. The Sabbath is arranged for the sake of man,
not the latter for the sake of the Sabbath. Man is master of the Sabbath too. If you had reflected on what I said to several members of
your estate on another occasion, namely that God demands love, not
sacrifices, you would not have reproached innocent people so severely."

In a synagogue on another Sabbath (Matt. 12:9–12), Jesus found
himself in the presence of a man whose hand had been injured. The
Pharisees, looking for grounds of accusation against Jesus, asked him
whether it is permissible to heal the man on this day. Jesus replied:
"Who among you would not rescue one of your sheep if it fell in
a ditch on the Sabbath! Well, how much more is a human being worth
than a sheep? So it's surely permissible to do good on the Sabbath."
—By now, as we have seen, there were numerous instances of ill will
on the part of the Pharisees against Jesus; indeed from this time on
they actually conspired with the party of Herod in order, if possible,
to do away with him.

At this point we find him back in Galilee where, seeking refuge
from his persecutors, he kept his whereabouts hidden and asked the
people who came to hear him not to make his presence known. From
among the throng of his listeners (Luke 6:12–13) Jesus singled out
a mere dozen as worthy of the special instruction that would enable
them to help spread his teaching. Realizing full well that the life and
energy of one individual would never be sufficient to educate an entire nation to morality, Jesus wanted to have at least a few into whom
he could breathe his spirit in its purity. Their names are . . . (see Mark
3:16–19).

Once (Luke 7:18), John sent several of his friends to Jesus so that
they might question him about the purpose of his teaching; Jesus
took the occasion to reproach the Pharisees for the indifference with
which they had greeted John's call to reform. He asked: "Is it some
sort of curiosity that has brought you out here in the desert? Surely

91 you're not here out of any desire / to make yourselves better. Perhaps
    you were looking for a man with no character, somebody who bends
    principles to his own advantage, a reed that blows with every wind?
    Or maybe you wanted to see someone all dressed up and living in
    high style? You don't find people like that in a desert; you find them
    in the palaces of kings! Or maybe you wanted to see a prophet or
    a miracle-man? —John was a good deal more than that! He found
    ready acceptance among the common people; but even he could not
    move the hearts of the Pharisees and the orthodox Scribes, nor make
    them receptive to goodness. With whom should I compare this sort
    of man? Perhaps with boys playing in the street, shouting to each
    other 'We played you a tune, but you wouldn't dance! Then we sang
    you sad songs, but you wouldn't cry!' Because he doesn't eat bread
    or drink wine, you say that John is bad-humored. But since I eat
    and drink like other people, you say 'The man is a glutton and a
    guzzler and associates with sinners.' —But wisdom and virtue will
    find their champions who will vindicate their worth."

    Despite this reprimand, a Pharisee named Simon invited Jesus to
    dinner. While he was there a woman who seems to have been greatly
    indebted to his teaching entered the room with a vessel full of pre-
    cious ointments and approached Jesus. The countenance of the vir-
    tuous one and her consciousness of her own sinful life made her tears
    flow and prompted her to throw herself at his feet. Realizing how
    much he had influenced her, how he had brought her to repent and
    return to the path of virtue, she kissed his feet and, drying the tears
    falling on them with her hair, she anointed them with a costly lo-
    tion. The graciousness with which Jesus accepted these gestures that
    helped comfort a contrite and appreciative heart, his kindness in not
    repelling them, offended the fastidiousness of the Pharisees. Their ex-
    pressions revealed their displeasure that Jesus was behaving so warmly
    toward a woman of such ill repute. Seeing this, he said to Simon,
    "I have a story for you." "Let us hear it," replied Simon. "A credi-
    tor," Jesus recounted, "had two debtors, one of whom owed him five
    hundred and the other fifty denares. Since neither was in a position
    to repay, he absolved them. Now which of the two loved him more?"
    "Probably the one," answered Simon, "whose greater debt he had
    remitted." "No doubt," said Jesus. And pointing to the woman he
    continued: "Look here. When I entered your house, you offered me
    no water with which to wash my feet. But she has washed them

with her tears and dried them with the locks on her head. You gave
me no kiss; but she did not regard it as / beneath her dignity even   92
to kiss my feet. You did not anoint my head with oil; but she anointed
my feet with costly salves. A woman capable of this kind of love and
gratitude is forgiven her transgressions, even if they were many; while
indifference toward such noble sentiments is no sign at all of a return
to the simplicity of virtue." And turning to the woman, Jesus added:
"It is a divine pleasure to behold the triumph of faith in your true
self, the confidence that you are still capable of goodness, and the
courage you have shown. Fare thee well!"

Moving on through other towns and villages (Luke 8), Jesus preached
wherever he went, accompanied by his twelve apostles; there were
also a number of women, some of them rich, who used their fortunes
to support the company. Once, in the presence of a large gathering,
he presented a parable. (A parable is a fictitious story that spells out
a specific moral lesson in sensuous form. Unlike fables, whose agents
are animals, and unlike myths, whose agents are demons and other
allegorical beings, parables have human beings as their principal
characters.) The parable went: "A farmer set out to sow seed. Part
of it fell on the pathway and ended up either trampled underfoot or
eaten by birds. Another part fell on rocky ground where it found
too little soil; although it sprouted, its roots were not deep enough
and it soon wilted in the heat. Still other seeds fell amidst brambles,
which shot up and choked them. But one portion fell on good land,
and bore fruit thirty-, sixty-, even a hundredfold."

When his disciples asked why he couched his teachings to the people in the form of parables, his answer was this: "Perhaps you are
capable of higher ideas concerning the kingdom of God and the morality
that affords free access to it. But experience has taught me that words
about these are lost on the Jews. Even while they insist on hearing
something from my lips, their deep-seated prejudices prevent the naked
truth from penetrating to their hearts. Whoever is in the least predisposed to internalize something better can profit from my teaching.
But those who lack this disposition will derive no use even from
what little knowledge of the good they already have. They have eyes
and see not, ears and hear not. This is why I address them only in
parable. But I will explain it to you.

"The sown seed is our knowledge of the moral law. Whoever has
the opportunity to attain this knowledge but does not grasp it firmly

is prone to having some seducer take from his heart what little goodness had been sown there. This is represented by the seed that fell along the pathway. The seed sown on rocky ground is also this / knowledge—which is indeed received with joy. But since it is not deeply rooted, it sways with each change in circumstance; and as soon as danger and misfortune pose enough of a threat, it simply perishes. The seed that fell among the brambles is the condition of those who, although they have heard of virtue, allow it to be smothered by life's cares and the deceitful seductiveness of riches, and thus remain without fruit. The seed that was sown on good ground is the voice of virtue that was fully comprehended and now bears fruit thirty-, sixty-, and even a hundredfold."

And he presented other parables too (Matt. 13): "The realm of goodness may be compared with a field whose owner had sown it with good seed. While its attendants slept, his enemy came, planted weeds amidst the wheat, and stole away. Later, when the seeds began to shoot up into sprouts of wheat, the weeds appeared as well. The servants asked their master, 'The seeds you sowed were pure; how is it that now there are so many weeds in the field?' 'An enemy of mine must have planted them,' the master replied. The servants asked, 'Do you want us to weed the field?' 'No,' responded the wiser lord, 'for along with the weeds you would also tear out the wheat. Just let them grow together until the harvest. Then I will order the harvesters to sort out the weeds and get rid of them, leaving only the pure wheat.'"

When Jesus was alone with his disciples, they asked him for an explanation of his parable; so he offered them this: "The sower of good seed represents those good persons who by their teaching and example make people aware of virtue. The field is the world. The good seed represents those who are virtuous, while the weeds are those who are wicked. The enemy who disseminates the weeds are seducers and their seductions. The time of harvest is eternity, the divine retribution for good and evil; here, however, virtue and vice are so closely intertwined that one cannot root out the latter without damage to the former."

And he described the realm of goodness in other ways, likening it to the mustard seed which, although tiny, grows into a plant so large that birds can nest in it; or to a little bit of yeast which, when kneaded into three bushels of flour, leavens the entire mass. "The kingdom of God fares like seed which, when sown in the soil, requires no further effort; it germinates and sprouts without our even noticing. For by nature the earth has its own germinating power, whereby the seed sprouts and shoots up into stalks bearing full fruit (Mark 4:26ff.)." /

He also compared the realm of goodness with a field containing buried treasure; when someone discovers it, he hides it again right away; elated, he sells all he has and buys the field. —And with a merchant looking for fine pearls; if he finds a particularly precious one, he sells his whole stock in order to come into possession of it. —And with a fisherman who has caught a bunch of fish in his net; sorting them out on shore, he puts the good ones in his bin, but throws the bad ones away. "So likewise at the time of the great harvest the good and the wicked will be separated from one another—the former by the reward they will find in the peace of mind that virtue brings, the latter by remorse, self-recrimination, and shame."

Once (Luke 8:19) when some of his relatives came to visit him, they found that they couldn't get very close to him because of the crowd of people around him. When Jesus was informed of this, he replied: "My true brothers and kinsmen are those who heed the voice of God and obey it." —On another occasion, receiving news (Luke 8:22; Matt. 14:13) of the murder of John, he had himself ferried to the eastern shore of Lake Tiberias; but he stayed only a short while among the Gadarenes (Luke 8:37) before returning to Galilee. Also at about this time (Luke 9) he sent his twelve apostles forth to follow his example and combat the prejudices of the Jews, who put their name and parentage (of which they were very proud, being in their eyes a sign of great privilege) above the value that morality alone bestows on mankind. "You don't have to make elaborate preparations for your journey," Jesus said, "or go out of your way to make your presence known. Wherever they are willing to listen to you, stay for a while. Whenever you are received unkindly, do not be insistent but leave the place at once and continue on your way." But they were gone only a short time before they were back with Jesus.

On one occasion Jesus found himself (Mark 7) among a group of Pharisees and scribes who had come from Jerusalem. These noticed that his disciples sat down with unclean (i.e. unwashed) hands; for according to a rule based on tradition, Jews never eat until they have taken care to wash. Moreover before each meal all drinking implements and other containers (even if they were already clean), as well as the chairs and benches, have to be rinsed. The Pharisees asked Jesus: "Why do your disciples / refuse to live in accordance with the rules of our fathers, and sit down to eat with unpurified hands?" Jesus replied: "There is a passage in your Scriptures that applies to you perfectly. It reads: 'These people pay me lip-service, but their hearts are far removed from me. Their worship has no soul, for it consists only in adhering to arbitrary rules of conduct.' You do not respect the divine law but give all your attention instead to human customs, such as purifying cups and chairs with water. In matters like these you are scrupulous; but you abrogate divine commandments in order to adhere to your ecclesiastical statutes. Thus for instance the law 'Honor your father and your mother; whoever utters unkind words to his father and mother must die.' You have replaced this with another law; according to you, if someone says in anger to his father or mother 'In the future anything that I might have done for you— anything good—will be dedicated to the temple instead,' then he is bound by oath never to do anything good for his parents again. And you even reckon it a sin if he does go ahead and do something for his father or mother. This is how you annul a divine commandment in favor of one of your own. And there are a number of other or- dinances that you have treated this way."

Then Jesus said to the crowd around him: "Listen to me and grasp what I say. No material thing, nothing which a human being takes in from outside, can defile him. Rather is it what he originates, what comes out of his mouth, that indicates whether his soul is pure or impure." And when his followers tried to tell him that the Pharisees were being scandalized by these utterances, he said "Let them take offence; the weeds that people plant have to be rooted out. It is the blind who are leading the blind. I want to save the people from such blind guides, lest they be led astray by the very ones they have en- trusted with their welfare."

When the crowd had dispersed and Jesus had gone back into the house, his friends asked him for an explanation of what he had said to the gathering concerning pure and impure things. "What!" Jesus exclaimed. "Even you have not reached the point of grasping it? Don't you understand that what enters a person's mouth simply goes into his stomach, gets digested, and then is eliminated as waste? But the words that come out of his mouth—indeed his actions as such—

95

spring from his soul, and these alone can be pure or impure, holy
or unholy. The soul, after all, is the source of evil thoughts and mur-
derous acts — of adultery and theft, of false witness and slander, of
envy and pride, of gluttony and avarice. It is these vices that desecrate
a person, not / his sitting down to eat without having purified his   96
hands with water."

When it was time for the Jewish Feast of Tabernacles (John 7),
his kinfolk urged Jesus to accompany them to Jerusalem so that he
might be heard and become known in an arena larger than any available in the villages and towns of Galilee. But he answered them that
the time was not right. They might go whenever they wished; the
populace did not hate them, for they, unlike him, had not confronted
the Jews with the corruptness of their customs and the evil of their
ways. Hence it was several days after his relatives had left Galilee that
Jesus, in total secrecy, went to Jerusalem. There people were already
inquiring after him, since as a Jew he had been expected to come.
And the opinion of the populace, particularly the Galileans, was divided
regarding him, with one segment considering him to be a righteous
man, and the other thinking of him as a seducer. Still, out of fear
of the Jews, the Galileans did not dare speak of him publicly.

Midway through the feast Jesus went to the temple and began to
teach. The Jews were taken by surprise at this, since they knew that
he had never received formal instruction. Jesus answered them: "My
doctrine is no human contrivance requiring painstaking effort on the
part of others to learn. Anyone who has resolved without prejudices
to follow the unadulterated laws of morality will be able to tell at
once whether what I teach is an invention of my own. Those who
pursue their own glory will of course attach great importance to human
speculations and precepts. But anyone who is truly concerned with
the glory of God has sufficient integrity to repudiate the inventions
that people have associated with the moral law or even put in its place.
I am well aware that you hate me and even have in mind to kill me
because I have said that it is permissible to cure a person on the Sabbath. Yet none other than Moses allowed you to circumcise people
on the Sabbath; all the more so, then, should you be permitted to
make them well!"

Some of the people of Jerusalem who heard him speak gave indication by their remarks that they had heard that the High Council
had resolved to have Jesus eliminated. They were surprised that he

spoke so openly and freely, and that no one had as yet seized him as planned. Jesus could hardly be the Messiah whom the Jews were expecting to come and restore the splendor of their religious worship and the independence of their state. For they knew whence Jesus had come, whereas according to the prophecies the Messiah would appear 97   as it were out of / nowhere. Thus the prejudices of the Jews placed them in constant opposition to Jesus. They had little use for a teacher who sought to reform their customs and to wean them away from their immoral prejudices. What they wanted was a Messiah who would free them from dependence on the Romans, and in Jesus they did not find anything of the sort.

The members of the High Council, informed by the police that Jesus was back in the temple, reproached them for not having taken him prisoner on the spot. And when they had presented their excuse, namely that they had never heard anyone speak like that and so had not dared to lay hands on him, the Pharisees retorted: "What! So he has seduced you as well? Do you see a member of the Council or a Pharisee who thinks anything of him? Only the mob which is ignorant of our laws lets itself be taken in by him." When Nicodemus, whom Jesus had once visited in the secrecy of the night, protested that according to the laws one cannot condemn a man without first hearing him out and obtaining accurate information about his actions, they accused him too of being a supporter of the Galilean. And surely no prophet would come from a place like Galilee to begin with. But evidently they could reach no formal decision concerning Jesus, for the Council adjourned.

Jesus spent the night (John 8) on the Mount of Olives — perhaps in Bethany, at the foot of the mountain, where he had some acquaintances. But he did return to the city and to the temple. While he was teaching there, the scribes and Pharisees brought him a woman who had been caught in an act of adultery. They thrust her down in the center of a circle as if to pass judgment on her, and put the case to Jesus. According to Mosaic law such a one is to be stoned to death. They then asked for his opinion. Perceiving their intention to ensnare him, he pretended not to have heard; then he bent down and began drawing figures in the sand with his finger. When they insisted on hearing his opinion, he rose up and said to them: "Let he among you who knows himself to be without fault cast the first stone at her." Then he started drawing figures in the sand again. In response to Jesus' answer the scribes began slinking away, one after the other, and soon he was left alone with the woman. Jesus then stood up and, seeing that no one was left but the woman, said: "Did no one condemn you?" "No one," she said. "Neither will I condemn you," he said. "Farewell, and do not stray again."

On another occasion (John 8:12–20), while Jesus was giving a public lecture in the temple, / the Pharisees demanded to know what   98
evidence he could produce to convince him or anyone else of the truth of his doctrines — they themselves having been blessed with a system of government and laws legitimated by solemn divine revelations. Jesus gave them this answer (John 8:21–31): "Do you really believe that the Deity threw the human species into the world and left it at the mercy of nature without a law, without awareness of the purpose of its existence, and without the possibility of discovering within itself how it might become pleasing to him?* You are certainly most fortunate that you alone have been endowed — for no apparent reason, in this one corner of the world and out of all the nations of the earth — with knowledge of the moral law. This must be what has all of your narrow, self-absorbed heads spinning. As for myself, I cling only to the untainted voice of my heart and conscience; whoever listens to these honestly receives the light of truth. And all I ask of my disciples is that they heed this voice too. This inner law is a law of freedom to which a person submits voluntarily, as though he had imposed it on himself. It is eternal, and in it lies the intimation of immortality. Obliged as I am to awaken men to this law, I, like any responsible shepherd, am prepared to give up my life for my flock. Perhaps you will take my life; but if you do, you will not be robbing me of it, because I offer it freely. You, however, are slaves. You stand yoked by a law imposed on you from without; and this is why you are powerless to wrest yourself free of bondage to your inclinations through self-respect."

From the way he had been received in Jerusalem (Luke 9:21ff.) and from the attitude of the Jews — especially their priests, who had resolved to excommunicate (i.e. exclude from religious services and public instruction) (John 9:22) anyone who regarded him as the awaited Messiah (which he had never openly claimed to be) — from all this

---

*Goethe: "Everyone understands it in whose bosom the spring of life flows pure." *Iphigenie* V, 3.

hostility he sensed the danger of violence, perhaps even that he would
be put to death. When he shared these thoughts with his disciples,
Peter remarked: "Let us hope that God isn't in favor of anything like
that!" But Jesus replied: "Oh? Are you so weak that you can't prepare for it—or perhaps you imagine me to be unready for it? Your
way of thinking—how rooted in sensuousness it is even now! You
99   still do not know the divine power that / comes from respect for
duty, a power enabling one to prevail over the inclinations and even
over the love of life itself." Then turning to the other disciples: "Anyone meaning to pursue virtue must be prepared to make sacrifices;
anyone intending to remain true to her must be ready even to give
up his life. Anyone who loves his life too much for that dishonors
his soul; but anyone who disdains it remains true to his better self,
liberating it from the sway of nature. What would it profit one to
gain the whole world and degrade himself in the process? What price
does one pay to reclaim lost virtue? The time will come when the
oppressed will radiate nobility, and reason, established in its rightful
place, will determine for every one the reward for his deeds."

Having stayed in Jerusalem longer than usual (from the Feast of
Tabernacles to the feast of the consecration of the temple in Decem-
ber) (John 10:22), Jesus returned for the last time to the setting where
his early life was played out, Galilee (Matt. 17:22). During this period
of his sojourn it appears that he no longer lectured to large crowds
(Mark 9:30), but occupied himself mainly with the education of his
disciples.

In Caparnaum (Matt. 17:24–27) the annual tax for the benefit of
the temple was demanded of him. "What do you think, Peter?" he
asked as he entered the [customs] house with him. "Do the kings
of the earth collect taxes from their own sons or from others?" "From
others," Peter said. "So the sons would be exempt," Jesus replied.
"And we, who worship God in the true spirit of the word, should
not have to contribute anything to the maintenance of a temple we
do not need in order to serve God, for we seek to do this by means
of a good life. But lest they be scandalized, and to avoid showing
contempt for what is so sacred to them, do pay it for us."

Among the disciples of Jesus a quarrel arose (Luke 9:46–50) concerning the rank appropriate to each, especially in the Kingdom of
God once it finally appeared. This stemmed from their continuing
to associate with it the most sensuous ideas, and from their still not

being entirely free of the Jewish notion of a worldly kingdom. They were not yet able to conceive the idea of God's kingdom purely as a realm of goodness, one in which reason and law alone govern. Jesus sadly listened to this quarrel, and then, having called a child to him, said to them: "If you do not change and return to the innocence, simplicity, and unpretentiousness / characteristic of this child, you   100 are truly not citizens of the kingdom of God. Anyone who feels antipathy toward others—let alone toward a child like this—or believes himself entitled to take something from them or treat them with indifference, is an unworthy person. But he who abuses the sanctity of innocence and damages its purity, he would be better off if someone were to hang a millstone around his neck and drown him in the sea. I know full well that this world will never relent in its attacks upon a pure sensibility; but woe to him who is the cause of such vexation! See to it that you despise no one, least of all the innocent at heart. This is the most delicate, the noblest flower of humanity— and the purest likeness of the Deity. This alone gives one stature, indeed the highest. Such simplicity is worth the sacrifice of all your fondest propensities: every impulse toward vanity and ambition, all false modesty, any concern with utility or advantage. —Only when you aspire to such simplicity, when you awaken to the dignity of which each person is capable and to which he is ordained, and when you finally realize that just as the same bark doesn't grow on every tree,[4] so differences of custom and manners do not matter, but in everything essential to human life whoever is not against you is in fact for you—only when you realize this will you not be subject to vanity and arrogance before others. —If you are nonetheless convinced that someone has really gone astray, try to improve him rather than be contemptuous of him; lead such a person to the path of virtue. What do you think? Will not a shepherd with a hundred sheep search all over the mountains in quest of a single stray? And if he has the good fortune to find it, will not his joy over this be greater than over the ninety-nine who did not stray?

"If someone does something to you, try to settle the matter between you. Bring him to account, and reach an understanding with him. If he listens to you and you cannot come to an understanding with him, it is your fault. If he does not listen to you, take one or

4. See *Nathan* IV, 4.

two others with you to help resolve the misunderstanding. If even this does not succeed, submit your dispute to the judgment of several arbiters. If he still does not offer you his hand in reconciliation, avoid him and have no further dealings with him. Insults and injustices which men forgive one another and seek to remediate are forgiven in heaven as well. When you thus unite in the spirit of love and reconciliation, then are you imbued with the spirit which I have sought to quicken in you." /

101 Hereupon Peter asked Jesus (Matt. 18:21-35): "How often must I forgive a person who offends me or does me wrong—up to seven times, perhaps?" "You think that anywhere near enough?" Jesus replied. "I would say, rather, up to seventy times seven. —Listen to a story. A prince wanted to settle accounts with his servants, and one of them, he discovered, owed him a debt of ten thousand talents. Since the fellow did not have this much, the prince ordered him to sell everything he could call his own, even his wife and children as slaves, and pay up. The man fell at his feet, imploring forbearance and a period of grace: he would repay all of it. The master, feeling sympathy with his plight, dismissed the entire debt. But as the servant was departing from his master, he met one of his fellow servants who owed him one hundred denares (a sum comparable to the previous as one to more than a million). Accosting him angrily, he vehemently demanded payment and, refusing to listen to the other's abject plea for patience, had him put in prison until the entire debt would be paid off. The other servants who witnessed the incident were appalled by this treatment, and reported it to the prince. He summoned the obstinate fellow, and said to him: 'Callous fool! At your pleading I forgave you an enormous debt. Couldn't you show to others anything of the mercy I had on you? Away with him!' And the prince commanded that he be kept in prison until everything was paid. —From this you see that reconciliation, forgiveness, is the mark of a purified disposition, which is all that our holy God readily accepts of our otherwise often faulty deeds. Only on this condition could you ever hope, in view of eternal justice, for release from the punishment which your previous way of life had merited—indeed only if your whole disposition is changed can you become different persons."

When he decided (Luke 9:51) to go again to Jerusalem, it was by way of Samaria. At one point on his way he sent several of his companions ahead to make necessary arrangements in a local town. But the Samaritans, perceiving their intention to travel to Jerusalem for the Passover, did not want to extend them their hospitality, and even refused them passage. So a few of Jesus' companions conceived the notion of imploring heaven to consume this town with lightning. At this Jesus turned to them indignantly: "Is this the spirit that animates you, the spirit of vengeance? A spirit such that, if the powers of nature stood at your command, you would use these to requite an unfriendly encounter / with destruction? Your aim is to cultivate the 102 realm of goodness, not to destroy!" Then they proceeded to go back.

When on the way (Luke 9:57), a scribe offered Jesus his services as a steady companion, Jesus cautioned him: "Note that while foxes have their dens and birds their nests, I have no place that I can call my own, no place to rest my head." Having started (Luke 10) on another, somewhat more roundabout way to Jerusalem, he again sent two of his companions ahead to prepare the people for his arrival, for his entourage was quite sizeable. And he instructed them that they should extort no favors, should continue onward whenever they were not wanted, and should concentrate at all times on inspiring the people to goodness—there still being so much left to do in this regard and the [number of] workers so few.

His disciples (Luke 10:17ff. —cf. Matt. 11:25–30) brought him the news that in some places they had been well received. At this, Jesus exclaimed: "Thanks and praise be to you, father of heaven and earth, that it is not the exclusive property of the erudite and the knowledgeable to recognize what everyone's duty is—that every uncorrupted heart can experience for itself the difference between good and evil. Oh, if only mankind had stopped at this, and had not, over and above the duties that reason enjoins, invented a host of vices with which to plague itself: vices which eventually become a source of pride, and in which no comfort is to be found other than at the expense of virtue!"

On this journey Jesus met a scribe who, in order to learn of his principles and examine them, engaged Jesus in a discussion. "What must I do, Master, to become worthy of blessedness?" "What does the law instruct you to do?" Jesus asked in reply. "You ought," the other answered, "to love the Deity as archetype of holiness with all your soul, and love your fellow man as though he were your own self." "You have answered well," Jesus said. "Adhere to this, and you will merit the highest happiness." The scribe wanted to show that this simple answer was not yet satisfactory for his deeper-searching soul: "What is still needed is a clarification of who exactly we are to regard as our fellow man, the ones we are commanded to love." "I will make this clear for you by way of a story. A man journeyed from Jerusalem to Jericho — a route that led through a desert and was unsafe. He fell into the hands of brigands who stole his clothes and

103   left him wounded and half-dead. By chance a priest came along / the same route right after this occurrence and saw the wounded man, but continued on his way. A Levite also came along this path, and passed him by without so much as a twinge of compassion. But a Samaritan who was travelling nearby took pity on him as soon as he saw him, and so went over to him, cleansed his wounds with wine and oil, and bandaged them. Then he took him on his mule to an inn where he had him looked after. Since he was planning to continue his journey the next day, he left the landlord a sum of money to pay for whatever the invalid might otherwise need, and even urged the innkeeper to spare no expense should the cost exceed this sum: he would make up the difference on his way back. — Now which of the three has proven himself to be the fellow man of the unfortunate?" The scribe: "The one who took a sympathetic interest in him." "So should you likewise," Jesus said, "look upon everyone who has need of your help or your sympathy as your fellow man — regardless of what nation, what faith, or what color he may be."

Now of course the Pharisees (Luke 11:16; Matt. 16:1) were quite unreceptive to the teachings of Jesus, who was always reproaching them for the moral inadequacy of their legalistic conduct. And they demanded of him on various occasions that his teaching, which denied the value of their legislation, be corroborated — perhaps by some sort of extraordinary atmospheric phenomenon, such as Jehovah had performed to back up some solemn proclamation. But Jesus gave them this answer: "In the evening you say that tomorrow's weather will be good if the sky has a fine sunset. But if the morning sky is dull red, you prophesy rain. Thus you are expert at predicting the weather from the way the sky looks. Yet you seem unable to evaluate the signs indicating the present state of things. Don't you perceive that higher needs have been awakened in man, that reason will keep pressing its claims against your arbitrary dogmas and precepts, your degradation of the purpose of human existence, your disparagement of virtue in mankind, and the coercive means by which you seek to maintain respect for your beliefs and commandments among your people? You

will be given no signs, only teachers; from these even you could learn
what would be best for you along with the rest of humanity."

On this occasion (Luke 11:37 – cf. Matt. 23) a Pharisee invited
Jesus to lunch. The Pharisee was surprised that Jesus did not wash
his hands before he sat down to eat. Jesus told him: "You wash the
outside of the cup and plate; but does that make the inside clean as
well? When / someone puts his external appearance in good order,   104
is everything [automatically] put right inside? Where the soul is sanctified, the exterior is sanctified too. You correctly give a tithe of mar-
joram and of rue and of every insignificant little herb that grows in
your garden. Amidst this scrupulosity over small matters, which you
pass off as perfection, aren't you forgetting that there are higher obligations? Justice, compassion, honesty: the observance of these constitutes the essence of virtue; and to practice them involves everything else that has to be done. But doesn't your notion of what has
value take only externals into account? You place so much importance on your rank in the lecture hall, on who is presiding at ban-
quets, and on who it is you are greeting in the street. You hinder
people with a host of burdensome rules, while you yourselves are ob-
sessed merely with appearances! You presume to be the keepers of
the key to the sanctity of truth, and yet you block the entrance to
it both for yourselves and for others by means of irrelevant ordinances."

These and stronger rebukes were directed by Jesus at the scribes
and Pharisees controlling the government of the land, and at their
sacrosanct customs – serving to embitter them increasingly and ripen
their resolve to bring some action against him.

Then before an enormous crowd of people (Luke 12) he spoke ur-
gently of the danger of allowing oneself to be infected by the spirit
of the Pharisees. "Beware," he said, "of Pharisaic ferment; although
it itself is not very noticeable and does not alter the outward appearance overall, it still gives an entirely different flavor – I am talking
about hypocrisy! Such dissemblance will not deceive the eye of the
one who sees all; before him the heart's disposition lies open, however much one may seek to hide it. Since he knows all, he alone has
no need to judge men by their deeds, by the outer manifestations
of character that are so often deceptive to us. He judges according
to the inner goodness of their will. – My friends, I tell you do not
be afraid of people whose power extends no further than to kill the
body. Fear rather the undermining of the dignity of your spirit, whereby

it is declared before God and reason that you deserve to lose your
true happiness. For it is hypocrisy of the worst sort when one refuses,
out of mortal fear, to express in action and acknowledge in word the
principles of truth and virtue. To speak ill of me or any other teacher
105   of virtue is a quite forgivable / matter; but to slander the holy spirit
of virtue itself is utterly depraved. Nor should you harbor any childish fear of embarrassment if you are called to account before tribunals
or in lecture halls because of your free avowal of the good. Motivated
by the spirit of virtue, you will lack neither the courage nor the words
to defend it."

Then one person in the crowd approached Jesus and, hoping that
his authority might be more influential than his own, implored him
to prevail upon his brother to share his inheritance with him. But
Jesus answered him: "Who made me the judge or arbiter between
you?" And turning to the others: "Do not give in to covetousness.
A human being does not fulfill his destiny by becoming richer and
richer. —Let me clarify by an example: A rich man's farms bore him
so much fruit that the sheer quantity of it became something of an
embarrassment to him, and in order to keep it all he had to enlarge
his barns. He thought to himself: 'That accomplished, you will take
care to maintain what you have and so have plenty to live on for many
years to come. You will rest, eat, drink, and be content.' But then
he heard the voice of Death: 'Fool! This very night your soul will
be taken from you. For whom have you been accumulating?'

"When one heaps up riches, giving no thought to one's destiny,
to such treasure as is suited to eternity, one's efforts are futile and
base. Preoccupation with riches cannot fulfill your soul; [for that]
your spirit has to be devoted to duty alone and your labors dedicated
to the realm of goodness. Only then will you stand as men: prepared
for living or for dying, no longer so attached to life that you are terrified of death even while this fear robs you of your vitality. Do not
put things off. Don't think that there will always be time later on
for devoting yourselves to purposes higher than self-indulgence and
the accumulation of wealth. Any time detracted from service for the
good is lost to your own destiny.

"Otherwise, as death approaches, you will be like the housekeeper
who, having been entrusted with taking care of things in his master's
absence, says to himself: 'My lord should be gone for quite some time,'
and so begins gorging himself, getting drunk, and taking advantage

of the servants. But when the master returns unexpectedly, he catches him totally off guard and metes out to him exactly what he deserves. —And just as the servant who knows his master's will and does not obey it shall be punished more severely than one who performs just as poorly but in ignorance of the master's will, so also shall much be expected from the person to whom much has been entrusted, the one with the talent and opportunity to perform much good. Do you really imagine that I have summoned you to a quiet / enjoyment of life? Or that a carefree and happy future is the destiny that I desire and expect? No! Persecution will be my lot, as it will yours! Dissension and strife will be the consequence of my teachings. The conflict between vice and virtue—between dependence upon the conventional opinions and customs proper to the sort of faith that some authority plants in the heads and hearts of the people, and a return to the service of reason established in her own right, the service which brings one back to life—this conflict will alienate friends and families. And it will vindicate the honor of mankind's nobler element. However, if those who overthrow the old ways that put fetters on the freedom of reason and pollute the springs of morality proceed only to replace it with another faith imposed by decree and bound by the letter— depriving reason once again of the right to derive the law from within itself, to believe in it and subject itself to it freely—then things will be worse than before. Woe to all if they then wield the sword of external power to promote this compulsory belief, thus inciting fathers against sons, brothers against brothers, mothers against daughters, and turn mankind into betrayers of humanity!"

Jesus was told (Luke 13) of an event that had taken place around this time: Pilate, the Proconsul of Judea, had ordered (no one knew for what reason) the execution of several Galileans while they were offering sacrifice. Familiar with his disciples' thinking (John 9) (for instance, when on another occasion they happened upon a man blind from birth, they leapt to the conclusion that either he or his parents must have been grave wrongdoers), he took the opportunity to admonish them. "Are you perhaps entertaining the notion that because they met such a fate these Galileans had to be the worst of their people? Perhaps, too, the eight or ten people in Siloam recently crushed by a [collapsing] tower were the most depraved of everyone in Jerusalem? No! To judge so callously is no way to regard those who meet with misfortune. You ought rather to be startled out of your com-

106

placency, ought to examine your conscience and honestly ask whether you yourselves haven't deserved such a fate. —Consider the following: A man who owned a vineyard planted a fig tree in it. But whenever he came to pick fruit from it, he found none. So he said to / his gardener: 'For three years this tree has been useless to me. Take it out and we'll make better use of the space.' The gardener replied: 'Give it a little while longer. I'll loosen the soil around it and work in some manure. Maybe I can get it to bear fruit. If not, I'll cut it down.' A well-deserved fate is oftentimes delayed in this way, giving the wrongdoer time to right himself and the negligent one time to learn of higher purposes. If, unconcerned, he lets this time slip away, then fate overtakes him and the vendetta strikes."

107

As he continued on his way to Jerusalem, stopping occasionally to give people counsel, Jesus was asked whether very many ever attain happiness. He answered 'Each individual struggles on his own to find the narrow path of a good life, and many who make the attempt miss it. But once the innkeeper has locked his doors, and you come knocking and calling out for him to put you up, he will answer that he does not know you. And if you then remind him of a time when you did eat, drink, and listen to his tales with the other guests, he will say: 'Yes, you ate and drank with me, and listened to what I had to say; but now you've turned so rotten that you're no friend of mine. Go away!' Thus many who hail from morning or evening, from noon or midnight, who worship Zeus or Brahma or Odin, will find favor; but among those who are so proud of what they know of God, yet whose lives do dishonor to this higher knowledge even as they imagine themselves to be first and best, many will be rejected."

A number of Pharisees took it upon themselves to warn Jesus (it is not known what their motives were) that he should leave Herod's domain, inasmuch as the King had designs on his life. Jesus' reply was that his activities were simply not the sort of thing that could alarm Herod, especially since it would be astounding if Jerusalem— the customary deathtrap for all the teachers who tried to cure the Jews of their obstinacy, their prejudice, and their deceitful violation of every principle of morality and wisdom—if Jerusalem wouldn't take care of things by dealing with him in the same way.

108

While dining with another Pharisee (Luke 14) Jesus noticed how / several of the guests were taken up with getting the most prominent seats, the ones they felt to be appropriate to their station. He observed that crowding into the most prominent seats might well occasion embarrassment, since if someone of still higher rank were to appear, one would have to give up one's place and move to an inferior one. But someone who went ahead and sat at the lower end of the table, and was called by the host to sit further up, would gain a measure of respect. In general the one who exalts himself is humbled, whereas the modest one is elevated. He remarked to the host that he knew of a kind of hospitality greater than that shown by inviting to dinner relatives, friends, and wealthy neighbors (all of whom usually reciprocate this demonstration of friendship by returning the invitation). He knew of another, nobler form of liberality: feeding the poor, the sick, the unfortunate—kindnesses that would receive no thanks except for unsophisticated expressions of gratitude, the relief the receivers experience from their misery, and one's own simple cognizance of having tended to the wounds of the unfortunate and brought help in time of need.

One of the guests shouted: "Happy is the man who is counted among the citizens of God's kingdom!" At this Jesus described the kingdom of God by portraying a prince (Matt. 22) who wanted to celebrate the marriage of his son at a grand banquet with many guests. "On the day of the feast he sent his servants to inquire of those who had been invited whether they were coming, for the banquet was ready. The first sent his apologies; he couldn't attend because he had to survey some recently purchased fields. The second couldn't come either, because he had to examine the five pair of oxen he had just bought. A third excused himself because he had only just now gotten married. Some others even treated the servants with contempt; and in short, none of the invited guests appeared. Exasperated, and in view of the expense already incurred, the prince ordered his servants to go into the streets and squares of the city and to invite the poor, the blind, the crippled—anyone who was ailing. The servants did this; but since there were still a lot of empty places, the master sent them out yet again, to search the streets and alleys and bring back whomever they found until the house was full. This is how it is with the kingdom of God as well. A lot of people put more importance on petty ends than on their higher destiny. Many whom nature or fortune has placed in a greater arena of action, irresponsibly neglect this opportunity / to do much good. And integrity is often   109
banished to lowly huts or left in the hands of limited talents. —But

one of the foremost characteristics of a citizen of the realm of goodness is the ability to sacrifice oneself. He to whom his relationship
as son, brother, husband, or father, he to whom happiness and life
are dearer than virtue, is not well suited to striving for perfection
or to leading others toward it. Whoever intends to work for others
is in special need of first testing his strength to see whether he is
capable of seeing this through. Otherwise he will be like a man who
starts building a house without figuring out the total cost ahead of
time; when he has to abandon the project unfinished, he becomes
a laughing stock. Or, just as any prince tests the strength of his forces
before he challenges a foe who threatens him with war, seeking rather
to negotiate if he finds his forces inadequate, so anyone who wishes
to dedicate himself to the betterment of mankind ought to test his
own mettle and find out whether he will be able in the course of
the struggle to renounce all that he would otherwise find alluring."

Again the Pharisees were shocked (Luke 15), this time because they
saw among Jesus' listeners a number of publicans and other disrepu-
table persons whom he would not banish from his midst. About this
Jesus remarked: "If a sheep strays from a shepherd's flock, isn't he glad
when he retrieves it? If a woman loses some of her money, doesn't
she search for it high and low, and after finding it, doesn't she seem
more delighted over this than about the money she didn't lose? Aren't
the virtuous likewise happier to see a wayward person return to the
path of virtue? —Let me tell you a story: A man had two sons. The
younger one asked for his inheritance, and so the father divided his
estate. After a few days this son packed his belongings and journeyed
to a distant land in order to enjoy his inheritance freely and in keeping with his own tastes; once there, he squandered everything in de-
bauchery. When famine struck his lot worsened and he found himself in direst straits. Eventually he was hired by a man who sent him
out into the fields to tend the pigs, with whom he had to share a
diet of acorns. His sorry plight made him think of his father's house,
and he thought to himself: 'My father's day-laborers are better off
than I am! They always have bread, while I am ravaged by hunger
here. I should go back to father and tell him: "Father, I know I have
sinned against heaven / and against you. I am no longer worthy of
being called your son. Please, just take me on as one of your labor-
ers."' When he went back, his father saw him coming from afar and
ran to him, embracing and kissing him. The son, contrite and miser-

able, said: 'Father, my failings have made me unworthy to call myself your son.' But the father ordered his servants to get him the best coat and give him shoes. 'And slaughter the most suitable calf. Let us all rejoice! My son, who was as good as dead for me, has returned to life. He was lost and has been found.' Meanwhile the older son returned from the fields. As he approached the house, he heard cries of joy and asked what was happening. When a servant told him, he became so angry he refused to go into the house. The father came out and remonstrated with him. But the son would have none of it. 'I have been with you for so long, have worked for you and followed your bidding in everything, and you have never offered to let me have a feast with my friends. Yet along comes this one, who squandered a fortune on loose women, and you order a celebration for him!' 'My son,' said the father, 'you are always at home. You want for nothing: everything that is mine is yours. You should rejoice and be in high spirits that your brother, who had gone astray, has taken himself in hand — that we have gotten back the one for whom we had lost hope.'"

On another occasion (Luke 16), of which we have no details, Jesus told his friends the following story: "A rich man's steward was denounced to him for having squandered the fortune entrusted to him. The master had him summoned and said to him: 'What is this I hear about you? Your post is at stake; I want a full account of what you have done as steward.' The steward was in a quandary over what to do; he was about to lose his position, he lacked the strength for day-laboring, and he was ashamed to beg. Eventually he hit upon a solution: he would ingratiate himself with his master's debtors so that, when it was time for him to surrender his position, they would take care of him. He called them in one at a time. He let the first, who owed one hundred barrels of oil, draw up another promissory note on which the debt was given as merely fifty barrels. Then he let the second reduce his debt of a hundred measures of wheat to eighty. And he did similarly with the others. The master, when he learned of all this, had to acknowledge at least the cleverness of the disloyal steward — in which regard good people are usually at a disadvantage, / since cleverness does not balk at dishonesty. — Now the moral I draw from this story is that the sagacity you invest in monetary matters should be devoted to making friends among the people, especially among the less fortunate — but not, as did the steward, at the expense of your integrity. For someone who is untrustworthy in little things

111

will be all the more so in matters of importance. If you cannot be honest in money matters, how will you ever become receptive to the higher concerns of mankind? If you are so attached to things apart from man that for their sake you are prepared to ignore virtue, can anything greater be expected of you? A life spent in pursuit of one's own advantage can never be reconciled with a life in the service of virtue."

Several Pharisees who heard this, and who were very fond of money, made light of the fact that Jesus was so disparaging of the value of riches. But he turned to them and said: "All that you care about is to maintain the semblance of piety in the public eye. But God knows your hearts. What looks great and worthy of esteem in your sense-bound judgment vanishes into its own nothingness before the Deity. —There was once a rich man who spent his days revelling in luxury, clothed in purple and silk. At his door there often sat a poor man named Lazarus, whose body was diseased and covered with sores that went untreated except for stray dogs coming up and licking him; and he often had to appease his hunger with no more than crumbs from the rich man's table. The poor man died and made his home in the land of the blessed. Then, not long after, the rich man died too, and was put in the ground with great ceremony; but the lot of the poor man was not to be his. Lifting his eyes he saw Lazarus in the company of Abraham and cried out: 'Oh Father Abraham, have mercy on me and send Lazarus so that he might relieve my torment with but a drop of comfort, just as one who is feverish is comforted by even a drop of water!' Abraham replied: 'Remember, my son, that you thoroughly enjoyed the good things in the other life, whereas Lazarus was miserable. He has solace now, while you suffer.' 'Then I ask only this, Father, that you send him to my paternal home. For I have five brothers there, whom he must tell of my fate and warn them lest they too should come to this.' 'Their own reason provides them with a law, and there is the counsel of good men for them to heed.' 'That is not enough for them' said the unfortunate one. 'But if a dead person were to appear to them out of the grave, then they would surely mend their ways.' Abraham replied, / 'Man is given the law of his own reason. No other instruction can reach him, whether it come from heaven or from the grave. For either one would be entirely repugnant to the spirit of that law, which demands a voluntary subjection, not a slavish one compelled by fear.'"

On another occasion (Luke 17:5) of which the details are obscure, Jesus' friends made a special request of him, namely that he inspire them to greater courage and resolution. But Jesus answered: "Nothing besides reflection on your duty and the great goal ordained for mankind could ever do what you ask. For thereby you will never find that your work is done, and will not imagine that you will eventually be entitled to enjoy yourselves. —When a servant comes home from the fields, his master doesn't say: 'Now you can go ahead and relax,' but rather: 'Go fix my dinner and serve it to me; after that you can eat too.' And when the servant has finished all his chores, the master does not think he owes him any thanks. The same holds for you. When you've done what you ought to do, do not think: 'We've put in extra effort; it's time now to relax and enjoy ourselves,' but rather: 'All that we have done is perform our duty.'"

Now Jesus often talked about the idea of the kingdom of God, and one day the Pharisees, who could never bring themselves to entertain anything but a sensuous representation of the divine kingdom, asked him when it was to come. Jesus answered: "The kingdom of God does not manifest itself in pompous splendor or in any outward way. No one can ever say 'Look! Here it is!' or 'That's it! Right there!' You have to understand that the divine realm can only be established within you." With this he turned to his disciples: "You too will often wish that you could see the kingdom of God built up here on earth. And often you will hear of some fortunate community where people abide by the laws of virtue. But do not chase after such mirages. Don't go looking for the kingdom in some outward union between men, however exemplary it might be—in a particular form of state or society, in the public canon of some church. The lot of the virtuous, the true citizens of God's kingdom, is persecution, not domestic order and prosperity. Indeed most often you will be persecuted· precisely by those who, like the Jews, are part of such a social order and are quite adept at maintaining it.

"Of any two individuals who profess the same faith and support the same church, one might be virtuous and the other a scoundrel. So don't be too taken by the outer look of things. However much it may serve your love of life and self-indulgence, don't let yourselves sink into complacency, presuming that because you've tended to the formalities you have / fulfilled your duty. Anyone who cannot sacrifice everything for the sake of his duty by that very fact becomes un- 113 worthy of the kingdom of God. —Nor should you allow (Luke 18) your perseverance to waver when you see your hope of accomplishing something good by your struggle fail to be realized again and again, deciding, from weariness and frustration, simply to drift along with the general current of corruption. Just as a plaintiff often finds his cause furthered not so much by the honesty of the judge as by his desire to be rid of the plaintiff's incessant pleas, so also you will accomplish much good through perseverance. When at last you comprehend the greatness of the goal which demands that you do your duty with all your heart, then your striving will be eternal, like the goal itself, and you will never weary, whether you see its fruits ripen in this life or not."

Regarding the Pharisees, who imagined themselves to be perfect and in their self-conceit held the rest of mankind in contempt, Jesus told the following story: "Two men went to the temple to pray. One was a Pharisee, the other a publican. The prayer of the Pharisee went like this: 'I thank you, oh God, that I am not like the rest of mankind—a thief, a scoundrel, an adulterer, or someone like that publican over there. I fast twice weekly. I attend services regularly. And I conscientiously tithe for your temple.' The publican stood far removed from this pious one, and did not dare lift his gaze toward heaven. Instead he beat his breast and implored: 'Oh God, be merciful to this sinner!' Let me tell you, when the publican went home, his conscience was more truly at rest than that of the Pharisee."

A young man of noble descent (Luke 18:18) approached Jesus. "Good teacher, what must I do," he asked, "in order to be virtuous and become worthy of eternal happiness in God's presence after this life?" "Why do you call me good?" Jesus replied. "No one is altogether good except God. And you know the precepts of your moral teachers: You shall not commit adultery, kill, or bear false witness, and you must honor your father and your mother." To this the young man said: "I have obeyed all of these commandments since childhood." "Then," said Jesus, "if you feel that you might be able to do still more, make use of your wealth to support the poor and to further morality, and become my helper in this." The young man heard this with distress, for he was very rich. Taking note of this, Jesus said to his disciples: "How tightly the love of wealth can entangle a person! How great an impediment to virtue it can / become for him! Virtue demands sacrifice, whereas love of riches dictates endless ac-

114

cumulation. The one requires self-containment, the other expansion, the endless increase of what he calls his own." The friends of Jesus asked him: "But how can we really have hope that such a basic drive as this will not prevent one from ever becoming virtuous?" "To counter such drives," Jesus replied, "virtue is endowed by God with a special law-giving force that imposes the obligation to achieve mastery over such drives at the same time that it provides us with the power to be able to do so." One of the friends, Peter, responded to this by saying: "You know that we have sacrificed everything in order to submit to your teaching and to devote ourselves to morality alone." "And for that," said Jesus, "your awareness that you have lived for duty alone is ample recompense — and not only in this life but in eternity."

Having arrived at the outskirts of Jerusalem (Luke 18:31; Matt. 20:17) with his little entourage of twelve chosen friends, Jesus shared his dark forebodings concerning the kind of reception he would be accorded there — presentiments very different from what his disciples expected regarding the entry into Jerusalem. Even those who were privy to Jesus' daily companionship and instruction had still not rid their Jewish heads of the sanguine expectation that he would soon make his appearance as king, restore the glory of the Jewish state and its independence from the Romans, and reward them, his friends and helpers, with power and honors for all that they had had to endure in the meantime. Such hopes had not as yet been dispelled, and they had not yet taken to heart the spiritual sense of the kingdom of God, its being the reign of the laws of virtue among men. Indeed the mother of John and James approached Jesus, fell at his feet, and, when asked what she sought, implored him together with her two sons (who believed they were about to have their expectations fulfilled): "When you establish your kingdom, raise my two sons to a position second only to yours." Jesus answered: "You don't know what you are asking! Are you prepared to go through with what is required in such an undertaking — to devote your lives to the betterment of mankind and to share in whatever destiny awaits me?" They answered, no doubt convinced that this would be a splendid experience: "Yes, we are / prepared." "Then," said Jesus, "do your duty, and calmly submit to your destiny. But do not expect to see the realization of any of the hopes expressed in your petition. Nothing but the purity of your disposition — which lies open to God, not to me — can determine your worth in the eyes of the Deity."

The rest of Jesus' friends became rather incensed over this request by the two brothers. Jesus instructed them: "You know that the lust for power is a passion as seductive as it is common in men. It is manifest in all spheres of life, great and small. You must rid yourselves of it. Out of mutual respect concentrate your efforts on kindness and service to each other—just as the purpose of my life is not to rule over others but rather to serve mankind even to the point of giving up my life." Because they, too, expected that his feelings and friendship toward them would afford them prominent roles in his rise to power, Jesus enlightened them through a parable concerned with the differences in personal worth: "A prince once set out from the land where he was sovereign in order to take over a distant land. Before he left, he entrusted ten pounds to each of his servants, ordering them to invest it wisely for him. But soon after, the citizens sent a delegation informing him that they no longer recognized his rule. When he returned to reclaim his throne, he first demanded of his servants that they give account of the use they had made of his money. The first one said: 'With the money you entrusted to my care I have made an additional ten pounds.' 'Good,' replied the prince. 'You have managed well with a small amount, and so I will put you in charge of a good deal more: I herewith transfer to you the governorship of ten states.' Another had earned five pounds with the money, and the prince had him administer five states. A third said: 'I am returning your sum intact; I have carefully preserved it. I was afraid to risk it on anything, for you are such a hard master, willing to take where you have not given and to reap where you have not sown.' 'Your own justification condemns you,' answered the prince. 'If you knew that I am a hard man, reaping where I have not sown, why did you not give your money to the money-changers? At least then you could have returned my money with interest. You are to return the money; it shall belong to the one who earned ten pounds.' Now the servants thought it strange that the one who already had ten pounds should receive this as well. But the prince told them: 'He who has made good use of what was entrusted to him will have still more added on. But he who makes poor use, or indeed / no use at all, of his endowment hereby makes himself unworthy of even what was originally given him. —And now bring me those who renounced their obedience to me, so that I may punish them.' Even as did the prince, so does God judge the merit of persons in accordance with the conscientious use they make of the powers bestowed on them, and in accordance with their obedience to the moral law under which they stand."

Jesus was now in Jericho, some six hours from Jerusalem; and once again, when he entered the house of a publican, the Pharisees expressed their disapproval. The publican's name was Zaccheus; he had wanted to see Jesus, and because of the crowd and his small stature, he climbed up a tree, only to be surprised with the honor of having Jesus pick his house for his resting place. Realizing what might be surmised about his character from the position he held, and feeling that Jesus would take a dim view of him, he told of how he had reformed his whole way of thinking: "Of the fortune I have made, I am giving half to the poor; and for those of whom I have taken advantage, I am replacing the damage fourfold." Jesus expressed his pleasure over this return to uprightness, and added that leading men to this path was his sole purpose on earth.

It was the time of Passover again (John 11:54) and most of the Jews had already arrived in Jerusalem; but Jesus remained for several more days on the outskirts, in a town called Ephrem located in Bethany (John 12). A banquet was given in his honor, and his friend, Mary, was present; she anointed his feet with costly ointment and dried them with her hair. Judas, one of the other apostles of Jesus and administrator of the funds of the group, made the observation that this ointment could have been put to better use had it been sold and the money distributed to the poor. Judas was actually wishing that he had gotten the money into his purse, and would certainly not have forgotten himself when it came time to distribute to the poor. But Jesus indicated to him that he might have refrained from hurting Mary with his reproach, had he perceived the genuineness of her affection—not unlike the love shown the dead when one embalms them. As for his professed generosity to the poor, he would have ample opportunity to display that on most any other occasion.

Meanwhile (Matt. 26:3) the High Council of Jerusalem, expecting that / Jesus, like all other Jews, would come to the feast, had 117 resolved to take him captive and contrive to have him condemned to death. But they agreed to postpone the sentencing until after the feast, fearing that his fellow Galileans might make an attempt to free him during the festivities. Accordingly (John 11:56–57) the High Council arranged to be notified the instant that Jesus set foot in the temple.

But for the first few days of the feast the ones assigned to this task were perplexed by their inability to find him anywhere.

Six days after the banquet mentioned above, Jesus left for Jerusalem. When he came within sight of the city, tears welled up in his eyes. "Oh, if you only knew what is needed for your well-being! But as things are now this is hidden from you. Your arrogance, your unshakable prejudices, your intolerance will provoke your enemies into marching against you; and they will surround you and harrass you on all quarters, until your state, your constitution—the very things you take such pride in—are annihilated, and you yourselves are buried in ruins. And you will endure this without any sense of honor, of having died in defense of a great and worthy cause."

Jesus rode (as is quite common in the Orient) on an ass. And a considerable crowd of people who knew him came out to greet and accompany him; they carried olive branches, and amidst cries of joy he entered the city. But he still stayed the night in Bethany, not Jerusalem (Luke 20). In the morning he returned, appeared publicly in the temple, and preached there. His enemies (Matt. 21:17) tried to maneuver him into a vulnerable position by asking sophistical questions. They were of course looking for a pretext on which to indict him, but were also trying to instill hatred of him in the people— whose presence made them nervous, especially in view of how large a crowd of them had greeted his arrival in the city.

Hence at one point, while he was sitting before a huge audience in the temple, they asked him by what authority he was exercising the office of teaching in public. Jesus said: "Let me ask you a question in turn. Was it zeal for truth and virtue or some other, selfish intention that motivated John to teach in public?" His questioners thought: "If we answer the former, Jesus will ask us once more why we did not listen to him; if we answer the latter, we will rouse / the people against us." So they answered that they did not know. "Well then," Jesus said, "I cannot answer your question either. But you be the judge, for once! A man (Matt. 21:28) who had two sons ordered one of them to go into the vineyard and work. He said that he would not go, but regretted it afterward and went. The father then ordered the other son to the same task; he readily consented, but did not go. Now which son proved himself to be obedient to his father?" They answered, "The first." "This is how it is," Jesus replied, "among you. People who were widely regarded as morally corrupt were in-

spired by John to listen to the voice of virtue. They are now superior
to you by the good character of their disposition—superior to you
who have the name of God constantly on your lips and who make
such a pretense of living only to serve him."

Jesus then presented them with another story, involving a man
who invested in a large vineyard. Having built walls around it and
made it secure, and having enlisted vintners to cultivate it, he set out
on a journey. At harvest time he sent workers to gather what the
vineyard had yielded. But the vintners mistreated them in every possible way—as also happened to a second crew sent by the owner. Thinking that at least they would respect his son, he now sent him. But
the vintners thought that he was the sole heir, and that by means
of his death they could obtain possession of the estate. So they mur-
dered him. "Now what will the master of the vineyard do?" Jesus
asked the bystanders. "He will punish the vintners with the severity
they deserve, and entrust the vineyard to other vintners from whom
he will receive its fruits properly." "In like manner," said Jesus, "did
the Jews have the good fortune to attain sooner than many other nations a worthy concept of divinity and the Deity's will concerning
mankind. But you are nonetheless failing to cultivate the fruit that
makes human beings pleasing in the eyes of God. You are thus sadly
deluded when you believe yourselves to be God's beloved solely because of this advantage. And it is in fact a crime to mistreat those
people who feel and profess that there is something higher which
gives human beings true value." —If they had only dared to do so
in full view of the populace, the members of the High Council who
had brought this reprimand upon themselves would have seized Jesus
on the spot.

Several Greek Jews (John 12:20) who had come to the feast wanted
to speak with Jesus; they sought out some of / his friends, appar-   119
ently in order to request a private audience with him. Jesus was evidently unenthusiastic, realizing that they would bring with them the
conventional notions about the Jewish messiah and would want to
commend themselves to him, their future king and lord of the Jews.
He then took the occasion to say to his disciples: "These people are
mistaken in supposing that my ambition is to proclaim myself a messiah of the kind they are waiting for—in believing that I personally
demand their service, or that I am in any way impressed by this opportunity to swell the ranks of my followers. If they but obey the

sacred law of their reason, then we are brothers—members of one and the same society. But if they take my purpose to be power and glory, then either they have a false idea of man's lofty destiny or believe that I do.

"Just as the seed planted in the soil must first decay in order that its germ may sprout into a stalk, I do not demand to see the fruits of what I labor for; my spirit has not fulfilled its destiny in the husk of this body. But should I become unfaithful to what I know to be my duty merely to save my life? With sorrow do I perceive the intention behind the attacks made against me by the leaders of the people. They fully intend to take my life; but should I on that account wish for or beg of God: 'Father, rescue me from this danger!'? No. My efforts to summon the people to the true service of God, to virtue, have led me to this pass, and I am ready to accept any consequences that follow. If this again contradicts your expectations of the messiah you await—that he isn't supposed to die—then life has grown so out of proportion and death become so terrifying to you that you can no longer make sense of the death of anyone who is supposed to merit your esteem. But do I demand special respect for my person? Do I demand that you believe in me? Do I seek to impose on you some standard devised by me for appraising and judging the value of men? No. Respect for yourselves, belief in the sacred law of your own reason, and attentiveness to the judge residing within your own heart—your conscience, the very standard that is the criterion of divinity—this is what I have sought to awaken in you."

Yet again, several (Luke 20:20) from among the Pharisees and supporters of the house of Herod were sent to Jesus in order to engage him in discussion in order that they might detect some grounds for complaint before the Roman authorities. If one is to appreciate

120 how insidious was the question / they intended to put to him, and how easily Jesus could have given offence in his reply either to the authorities or the prejudices of the Jews, one must recall the Jewish turn of mind, which found it utterly intolerable to pay taxes to an alien prince, since they wanted to reserve any such for their own God and his temple. Those who had been sent to him addressed him as follows: "We know, Master, that you are forthright in whatever you say, that you hold to the unvarnished truth, and that you never say anything merely to please somebody. Tell us, is it right that we pay taxes to the Roman emperor?" Jesus, perceiving their intention, re-

plied: "You hypocrites, why are you trying to trap me? Show me a denarius. Whose picture is this, and whose inscription (legend)?" "Caesar's." "If you grant Caesar the right," said Jesus, "to coin money for your use, then you should give to Caesar what is his — and give to God whatever is required to serve him." They had to put up with this answer, inasmuch as they could not find a single thing wrong with it.

Another Jewish sect, the Sadducees, who did not believe in the immortality of the soul, also wanted to challenge Jesus with their views; so they said to him: "According to our laws, a man whose brother dies childless must marry the widow he leaves behind. Now it so happened that a woman married seven brothers in a row in this fashion (with each of them dying without producing children by her). If mankind were to continue existing after death, which one would she belong to?" To this absurd query Jesus replied: "In this life people do indeed marry. But once immortal beings have joined the company of pure spirits they shall have left such necessities behind with their bodies."

A Pharisee who had heard Jesus answer these questions so well ventured to ask one of his own (evidently without malice) concerning the highest principle of the moral law. Jesus responded: "There is one God, and him you should love with all your heart; to him you should dedicate your will, the whole of your soul, indeed all of your powers. This is the first commandment, and there is a second that is no less binding; it says, Love every person as though he were you yourself. There is no higher commandment." The Pharisee marvelled at the excellence of this response, saying: "You have answered in keeping with the truth. To devote one's entire soul to God and to love one's fellow man as one's own self is worth more than any sacrificing or burning of incense!" Jesus was delighted by the sound attitude of this man, and said to him: "In this frame of mind you are not far from being a citizen of the kingdom of God, where there is no such thing as seeking his favor through sacrifices, expiation, lip-service, or indeed any sort of renunciation / of reason."   121

In one corner of the temple (Luke 21:1) a collection box had been set up in which people placed gifts for the temple. Among those who contributed, including the rich who were giving rather large sums, Jesus observed a poor widow who deposited two farthings. He said of this: "She has put in more than all the others; for all of them contributed from their surplus, whereas she with this little gave her entire wealth."

Provoked by the attempts (Matt. 23) made against him by the Pharisees, Jesus took the occasion to warn his friends and the populace about them. "The Pharisees and scribes," he said, "have placed themselves on the throne of Moses. Although you should obey the laws that they order you to obey, do not follow their example, the way that they do things. Even though they administer the laws of Moses, they do not themselves obey them; the only purpose of their actions is to maintain the mere semblance of righteousness before the people. —[You Pharisees!] You consume the goods of widows and ingratiate yourselves with them by pretending to pray with them. You are like whited sepulchres whose exterior is painted over and whose insides harbor putrefaction. On the outside you give yourselves the semblance of holiness, but within there is hypocrisy and injustice." —And he went on to recount a number of other things about them that he had singled out for criticism on previous occasions.

As they were walking through (Matt. 24) the different parts of the temple, Jesus' friends commented on its splendor; but Jesus expressed his apprehension that this whole pompous way of worship, buildings and all, would come to an end. This made a deep impression on them, and so later, when they were alone with him on the Mount of Olives, from which they could see the priceless structures of the temple as well as much of the city, they asked him: "When will what you told us earlier actually happen? And what are the signs that will let us know that the messiah's kingdom is about to be realized?" Jesus answered them: "This expectation concerning a messiah will visit great tribulation on my countrymen, and, together with the rest of their prejudices and blind obstinacy, will set the stage for their total undoing. This chimerical hope will make them playthings in the hands of cunning betrayers and mindless enthusiasts. Take heed lest even you be led into this kind of error. You will often be told that here or there the awaited messiah has come; there will be many who will put themselves forth as such. And under this title they will proclaim themselves leaders of rebellions and heads of religious sects. They will venture prophecies and, as best / they can, perform miracles designed to bedazzle even good men. It will often be said that the long-awaited messiah is in the desert, or that he is hiding himself here among the graves. Do not be seduced into chasing after him. Such presumptions and rumors will give rise to political unrest and religious schism. People will take sides and in this partisan spirit will come to hate and betray one another. In their blind fanaticism for mere names and words they will believe themselves justified in abandoning the most sacred duties of humanity. The destruction of the state, the dissolution of all bonds of society and civility, and in their wake famine and pestilence, will make this unhappy land the easy prey of external enemies. Woe to pregnant women and infants then!

"During these hard times don't let yourselves be seduced into partisanship. There will be many so crazed and infected by such fraud that they won't even know how they got into such a state; caught up in the whirlwind, their every step will carry them further from moderation, and in the end they will find themselves so hopelessly involved in crimes that they will ruin even their own party. Get out, if you can, from any such arena of chaos and malice; abandon your home, and don't dally in order to attend to this or salvage that. No matter what, remain true to your principles. If the spirit of fanaticism prevails, preach moderation and exort love and peace. Shun religious and political parties; have no faith in their cabals or indeed in any association that vows in the name and belief of some one person to see a divine plan realized. Divine plans are not confined to a single people or faith, but embrace the entire human species with unpartisan love. Only when reason and virtue instead of names and slogans are recognized and practiced all over the earth may you declare the divine plan to have been accomplished. It is unwavering loyalty to this hope for mankind, not to the vain nationalistic hopes of the Jews, that will keep you free of sectarian sentiment and keep you forever upright and courageous. Indeed amid such conflicts your peace of mind and your courage must be founded on unadulterated virtue. Be alert lest a false complacency steal its way into your heart — complacency resting on your adherence to dogmatic formulas, lip-service, and on meticulous observance of the ceremonies of some church. Think what such a state of mind would be like: Ten virgins were waiting with their lamps for the bridegroom to come and take the bride home with him. Five of them had wisely provided themselves with ample oil, but the other five had foolishly neglected / to do 123 so. Late in the night, after a long wait, the bridegroom finally approached; now they all wanted to meet him, but the five who had no oil could not borrow any from the others (who only had enough for themselves) and so had to hurry off to buy some. While they were gone the bridegroom appeared, and the five wise ones accompanied him into the house for the wedding feast. But the others, who were counting on their invitation but had neglected the essential thing, were excluded. —So do not imagine it sufficient to have adopted some creed if you have neglected what is most necessary, the practice of virtue. Do not imagine that it will do, when you find yourselves in dire straits or on the verge of death, to recall hastily a few maxims of good conduct or adorn yourselves with merit gained from elsewhere; indeed each can have only enough merit to get by for himself, and is in no position to merit anything for someone else. Your creed and all your vain hopes of merit by external means will not hold up before the sacred judge of the world.

"I compare God's tribunal with that of a king who assembles his people and, as a shepherd separates the goats from the sheep, sorts out the good from the bad. To the good he says: 'Come, my friends. Enjoy the good fortune of which you have made yourselves worthy. For I was hungry and you gave me food. I was thirsty and you gave me to drink. When I was a stranger among you, you took me in. When I was naked you clothed me. When I was sick you cared for me. And when I was in prison you visited me.' Filled with astonishment, they will ask: 'Lord, when did we see you hungry or thirsty, so that we might have tended to you, or naked or a stranger, sick or in prison, so that we might have clothed, taken in, or visited you?' And the king answers them: 'What you have done for the least of my brethren and yours, this I reward as though it had been done for me.' To the others, however, he will say: 'Receive the reward for your deeds: Get out. When I was hungry or thirsty, you neither fed me nor gave me drink. When I was naked or sick or imprisoned, you cared nothing for me.' And these, too, will ask: 'When did we see you hungry or thirsty, naked or sick or in jail, so that we might have been able to do something for you?' But the king will give them a like answer: 'What you have not done for the least of them, I requite as if you had neglected to do it for me.' —This is how the judge of all the world condemns those who honor the divine one only with their lips and pious expressions rather than in their reflection [of him], their humanity."

Jesus was spending the daylight hours in the buildings and court-

yards of the temple, and his nights outside the city near the Mount / of   124
Olives. The High Council did not dare to carry out publicly its intention to incarcerate him. Thus nothing could have pleased them
more than the offer of Judas, one of the twelve most trusted friends
of Jesus, to reveal to them in return for money where Jesus would
be that night, and to assist them in secretly arresting him. Avarice
appears to have been Judas' ruling passion, and seems not to have
given way to a better disposition even through his intimacy with Jesus; it may well have been his original reason for becoming a follower
of Jesus (i.e. his hope that it would be satisfied when Jesus established
his messianic kingdom). When Judas realized that such a kingdom
was not Jesus' purpose, and that his own hopes had been delusory,
he sought, by means of betrayal, to salvage what he still could from
his friendship with Jesus.

In keeping with the custom of the Jews in Jerusalem, Jesus had
a Passover meal prepared at which mutton was the choicest dish. This
was the last evening that he spent with his friends, and he devoted
it entirely to them in order to engrave it in their memories. At the
beginning of the meal (John 13) Jesus stood up, removed his outer
tunic, tucked up his robe, and washed the feet of his friends with
a linen cloth — a service usually performed by domestic servants. Peter
did not want to let this go on; but Jesus told him that he would
find out the reason presently. When he was finished with all of them,
he said: "You have seen what I did; I, whom you call your master,
have washed your feet. I did this to show you how you should treat
one another. Princes (Luke 22:25), who love grandeur, let themselves
be called benefactors of humanity. Do not do likewise. Let none of
you elevate himself above another or take anything for himself at another's expense; rather should you all be as friends, kind and consid-
erate. Do not do your duty condescendingly, as though you were
doing someone a favor. — But then, you know all this already, to
your good fortune, if only you act accordingly. — However, I am now
not speaking to all of you. Rather must I invoke the saying: 'Someone with whom I am breaking bread kicks at me.' For one among
you will betray me."

This realization saddened Jesus and perplexed his friends. John, who
was nearest Jesus, asked him quietly which one it was. Jesus said to
him: "It is the one I give this piece of bread"—which he passed to
Judas, saying: "What you mean to do, do soon." Nobody else / under-   125

stood what this was supposed to mean, and thought that it had to do with some errand, since Judas managed the group's funds. Judas, however, saw that his intentions were not unknown to Jesus, and, perhaps fearing that he might be publicly disgraced or that remaining in Jesus' presence might weaken his resolve, hastily left the group.

Jesus then had more to say. "My loved ones, soon your friend will have fulfilled his destiny, and the father of mankind will receive him into the dwelling place of his happiness. In just a little while I shall be torn away from you. What I leave you is the commandment to love one another and the example of my love for you. Only through this mutual love are you to distinguish yourselves as my friends." Peter then asked Jesus: "Where are you intending to go that you would want to leave us behind?" But Jesus said: "On the path I take, you cannot accompany me." "Why," Peter replied, "should I not be able to follow you? I am ready to do so at the risk of my life!" "You want to sacrifice your life for me?" said Jesus. "I know you too well; you do not yet have the strength for it. But even before it is morning again, you will have the opportunity to test your mettle. —Do not be dismayed over my impending separation from you. Honor the spirit that dwells within you. Through it you learn to know the will of the divine one and the role of your species; only in this spirit does the path to truth and divinity open up to you. Listen to its unadulterated voice. Although our persons are distinct and separate, our essence is one, and we are in no way remote from each other. Up to now I have been your teacher, and my presence has guided your actions. But now that I depart from you, I am not leaving you behind as though you were orphans; I leave you with a guide within yourselves. The seed of goodness that reason has sown inside you I have awakened in each of you, and the memory of my teaching and love for you will sustain in you this spirit of truth and virtue—a spirit which people do not embrace only because they are ignorant of it and do not search for it within their souls. You have become men, able at last to trust in yourselves without having need of external restraints. Once I am no longer with you, your developed moral sense shall be your guide. Honor my memory and my love for you by pursuing the path of integrity on which I have led you. The holy spirit of virtue will keep you from stumbling; it will instruct you further in matters to which you have thus far not been receptive, and will recall to your memory and give meaning to much that you have not yet understood. I leave you / my blessing — not a meaningless salute, but a salutation rich in the fruits of goodness. My departure is to your advantage, because only through your own experience and practice will you achieve independence and learn to govern yourselves. My leaving you should fill you not with sorrow but with gladness, for I embark on a higher course in better worlds, where the spirit soars more uninhibitedly toward the fountainhead of all goodness and enters into its homeland, the realm of the infinite.

"With great anticipation did I look forward to the pleasure of this meal in your company. Let the dishes and goblets be passed round; let us renew here the bond of our friendship." Then in the manner of the Orientals (or the Arabs, who to this day promote lasting friendship by sharing the same piece of bread and drinking from the same chalice), Jesus served bread to each of them; and after the meal he had the chalice passed round, taking the occasion to say: "When you dine like this in friendship, remember your old friend and teacher. And just as our Passover meal commemorated that of our ancestors in Egypt, and the blood commemorated the sacrificial blood of the covenant in which Moses (Exod. 24:8) established a bond between Jehovah and his people, so in the future when the bread is passed, remember that he sacrificed his very body; and when the cup of wine is passed, remember the sacrifice of his blood. Remember me as the one who gave his life for you; and may your recollection of me, and of my example, serve you as a powerful stimulus to virtue. I look upon you as the shoots of a grapevine that have born fruit thanks to the nourishment they have received from it — shoots that will soon bring the good to fruition by virtue of their own vital energy. — Love one another. Love all men as I have loved you. The life I give for the benefit of my friends is proof of my love. I no longer call you disciples or pupils; these obey the will of their mentor, often without knowing the reason why they must act as they do. You have ripened into the independence characteristic of maturity, into the freedom of your will. You will bear fruit on the strength of your own virtue if the spirit of love, the power that inspires both you and me, is equal to the task.

"If you are persecuted or abused, recall my example; neither I nor thousands of others have fared any better. If you were to side with the accepted vices and prejudices, you would find plenty of friends; but as friends of the good, you will be hated. The life of an upright

individual is a standing reproach to the evildoer; he feels this and becomes embittered. And / if he can find no plausible pretext for per-
secuting the individual who is good and free of prejudice, he will
make the cause of prejudice, repression, and depravity itself God's cause,
persuading himself and everybody else that in his hatred he is acting
in the service of divine goodness. But the spirit of virtue, shining
upon you like a ray from other worlds, will inspire and lift you above
the petty and vicious purposes of men. —I say all this to you before
it happens, so that you will not be taken by surprise. But just as the
fear of a woman in labor is transformed into joy as she brings a human being into the world, so also will the trouble that awaits you
in time change into joy."

Then Jesus lifted his eyes toward heaven. "My father," he said, "my
hour has come, the hour in which I am to manifest in its complete
dignity the spirit whose source is your infinity, the hour in which
I return home to you! This destiny is eternity and lifts one above
everything that has a beginning and end, everything that is finite.
My vocation on earth—to know you, father, and the kinship of my
spirit with you, to do honor to myself through fidelity to this kinship, and to ennoble humankind by the awakened consciousness of
this dignity—this vocation on earth I have fulfilled. My love for you
has brought me friends who have come to realize that I never wanted
to impose anything arbitrary or alien on mankind, but have instead
taught only your law which silently dwells, however misunderstood
by most men, within each and every heart. My intention was not
to secure honor for myself by means of something original or distinctive, but to restore the self-respect that a degraded humanity had lost;
and I take pride in seeing that the characteristic common to rational
beings, the inclination toward virtue, has become everyone's endowment. Most perfect one, keep them such that love for the good be
their highest law, governing them from within. Only thus will they
be one, and remain united with you and with me. I come to you
with this prayer so that the joyous feeling that quickens me might
flow through them as well. I have made your revelation known to
them, and because it has moved them, the world hates them as it
does me for having responded to it. I do not ask you to deliver them
from the world—no such entreaty can be brought before your throne
—but to consecrate them by means of your truth, which shines forth
only from your laws. The high calling that I have undertaken, to edu-

cate men to virtue, I now entrust to them. May they in turn see it through, teaching their friends to stop kneeling before idols and to make virtue and their likeness to you, the holy one, the sole bond of their unity rather than mere words and beliefs." /

When he finished speaking, the whole company got up and left 128 Jerusalem as usual, now that night had fallen. They crossed over Kidron Brook to a farm house called Gethsemane, near the Mount of Olives (Luke 22:39). This place was known to Judas, since he had often stayed with Jesus there at night. Jesus asked his disciples to wait together while he went with three of them to a more remote place in order to be alone with his thoughts. Here for a time nature exacted its due. The thought of his friend's betrayal, the injustice of his enemies, and the harshness of the destiny that awaited him overtook him in the loneliness of the night, affecting him profoundly and filling him with dread. He implored his disciples to stay by his side and keep watch with him, and then began pacing back and forth agitatedly, talking to them a few times and waking them up whenever they fell asleep. Occasionally he stepped aside to pray: "My father, if it be possible, spare me the bitter cup that awaits me! But may your will, not mine, be done. If there is to be no reprieve for me in this hour, I resign myself to your will." Sweat poured from him in large drops. No sooner had he rejoined his disciples and urged them to be watchful than he noticed some people approaching him. "Wake up!" he shouted to his disciples. "We must go; my betrayer is coming!"

Judas approached with several armed men, some of them carrying torches. Jesus, having renewed his determination, went to meet them. "Who are you looking for?" he asked. And they said, "Jesus the Nazarene." "I am he," Jesus answered. They were momentarily confused as to whether they had the right man. He asked them again and gave the same response, adding: "If it is me you seek, spare these who are my friends." Judas now stepped closer and gave his companions the prearranged sign for identifying Jesus, saying "Greetings, Master!" while he embraced him. At this Jesus said: "Friend, are you betraying me with a kiss?" The soldiers then seized him. Seeing this, Peter drew his sword and struck at random, cutting off the ear of one of the high priest's servants. But Jesus restrained and rebuked him, saying: "Stop! Respect the destiny that the divine one has ordained for me." And then, as they saw him being arrested, tied up, and taken away, Jesus' friends fled in all directions—all except a youth

who, having been startled out of his sleep, had in haste thrown on
only a cloak, and was now wanting to follow Jesus. But the soldiers
129   grabbed him, / and he saved himself only by slipping out of the cloak,
leaving it behind in their hands. On the way, Jesus said to his captors:
"You come to me armed as though you were seizing a brigand. But
you didn't arrest me publicly when I was sitting with you in the
temple every day. Midnight is your hour; darkness your element."

After having been first brought to Hannas, the old high priest
and father-in-law of Caiaphas, Jesus was brought before Caiaphas himself, who was high priest this year. The entire High Council of Jerusalem had gathered to receive the captive, and Caiaphas had impressed
on them the principle that they were duty-bound to sacrifice one for
the good of the entire people. — Peter, meanwhile, had followed the
apprehenders at a safe distance and would not have dared to set foot
in the palace itself had not John, who was well acquainted with the
high priest and had free access to his house, told the doorkeeper to
let Peter in. But she asked Peter: "Aren't you one of the followers
of this man Jesus?" Peter flatly denied it, and slipped in among a
group of ushers and servants keeping themselves warm by a fire.

Jesus was now before the high priest, who interrogated him about
a number of his doctrines and about his disciples. Jesus said: "I have
spoken freely and openly before everyone. I have taught in the temple
and in the synagogues frequented by all Jews. And I have no secret
doctrines. So why do you question me? Ask those who have listened
to me what it is I have taught. They will be able to tell you." One
of those who had arrested him thought Jesus' answer impudent. "So
this is how you respond to the high priest!" he said, and struck Jesus.
Jesus calmly said to him: "If I have not answered correctly, tell me
where I am wrong; but if I have answered well, why do you hit
me?"* Many witnesses were summoned to testify against Jesus. But
the priests could make no use of it, since their testimony was neither
conclusive nor consistent enough. Finally several came forward who
testified that they had heard Jesus speak disrespectfully of the temple;
but even these did not concur regarding his exact words. Jesus greeted
all of this with silence, until at last the high priest stepped forth im-

---

*According to John 18:24, this appears to have happened in the palace of Hannas.
But if the Council was gathered at Caiaphas' house, with the actual interrogation
taking place there, this does not coincide with the place where Peter denied Jesus.
—At Caiaphas' house alone? But it says everywhere *archiereis* in the plural.

patiently and said: "Do you have nothing to say about any of these accusations? Then in the name of the living God I order you to tell us whether you are / a holy man, a son of the Deity." "Yes, that is what I am," Jesus replied. "And one day you shall see this despised individual, to whom the Deity and virtue were sacred, arrayed in splendor and exalted above the stars." The high priest tore his robe and cried: "He has blasphemed against God. What need have we for further testimony? We have heard it straight from him! What is your opinion?" "He has condemned himself to death," was their judgment. This pronouncement was a signal for the ones who had arrested Jesus to begin mocking and abusing him; the High Council dispersed for a few hours, not to reconvene until early morning, and Jesus was left in their hands.

While this was going on Peter had remained by the fire (Mark 14:66ff.). But another woman employed by the high priest recognized him and said to the bystanders: "This is one of the companions of the prisoner. I am certain of it." Peter again answered with an unqualified denial. But a loyal servant of the high priest, in fact the one whom Peter had wounded a few hours earlier, said: "Didn't we see you with Jesus at the farm house?" The others concurred; moreover, Peter's dialect gave indication that he was from Galilee. Confronted all at once with so much that testified against him, Peter, desperate and afraid, so forgot himself that he protested to high heaven and swore that he did not know what they were talking about — that he was totally unacquainted with the person they said was his friend. At that moment the roosters began to herald the dawn, and in the midst of Peter's protestations Jesus, who was being led past him, turned in his direction with a penetrating glance. Peter felt this deeply, and realized at once how contemptible his behavior had been. He knew now how justified Jesus had been during the conversation of the previous evening in doubting Peter's resoluteness in the face of adversity — the very thing in which he had taken such pride. He quickly withdrew and shed bitter tears of shame and remorse.

When the few remaining hours of night had passed, the High Council reassembled. Its verdict was death. But since it was no longer legally empowered to pass such a sentence and carry it out, the assembly proceeded that very morning to take Jesus before Pilate, the Roman governor of the province, in order to hand him over lest there be any sort of uprising while he was still in their hands. —As Judas,

130

the traitor, came to realize that things had gone so far as to entail Jesus' condemnation to death, he regretted his action. He brought the money (thirty pieces of silver) back / to the priests and said: "I have done wrong in delivering this innocent man into your hands." But he was told that his action was no concern of theirs, whereupon Judas threw the money into the temple's collection box and went out and hanged himself. The priests had scruples about adding this money to the temple's coffers, since it was blood money; so they used it to buy a plot of land which they designated as a burial place for foreigners.

131

The Jews did not enter Pilate's palace lest they be defiled—it still being a feast day. Pilate went out to the courtyard and asked: "Of what crime are you accusing this person whose condemnation you demand?" "Were he not a criminal, we would not have delivered him to you," the priests replied. Pilate answered: "Well then, put him on trial and prosecute him according to your laws." "But we are not allowed to pass a death sentence," they rejoined. When Pilate heard that the crime was supposedly deserving of the death penalty, he could no longer refuse to be the judge in Jesus' case, and so he had the Council's charges read to him. Now although in the eyes of the Jews Jesus' declaration that he was son of God was blasphemous—indeed a crime fully deserving of death—the Jewish Council realized that such an accusation would never elicit a death sentence from Pilate. Hence they accused Jesus of passing himself off as a king, and of leading the people astray, arousing in them an indifference toward the established law that would in the end lead them to refuse to pay tribute to the emperor. When Pilate had heard these charges he withdrew into the palace, summoned Jesus, and asked him: "Do you really claim to be the king of the Jews?" Jesus asked him in turn: "Do you yourself think that I would make such a claim, or do you ask me this only because others have accused me of it?" Pilate answered: "Am I a Jew, that I for my part should be waiting for a king of your nation? Your people and your high priests have brought this accusation before me; what have you done to provoke them into doing this?" Jesus replied: "They accuse me of laying claim to a kingdom. But mine is nothing like what people ordinarily have in mind when they think of a kingdom. If it were, I would have subjects and supporters who would have fought for me and kept me from falling into the hands of the Jews." "Then you do after all," Pilate retorted, "give yourself out to be a king, since you speak of a kingdom." "If you insist on calling it that, then yes," Jesus answered. "I believe myself born — and saw it as my destiny in the world — to teach the truth and to enlist disciples / in its cause. And those who love it have heeded   132 my voice!" "What is truth?" Pilate asked with the air of a courtier who shortsightedly yet smilingly condemns any seriousness of purpose. And there is little doubt that he regarded Jesus as a fanatic prepared to sacrifice himself for a word — for some abstraction that could have no meaning in his own soul. He regarded the entire affair as having to do exclusively with the religion of the Jews and not at all as involving a crime against civil law, let alone as posing a threat to the security of the state.

Pilate left Jesus, went out to the Jews, and told them he could find nothing to charge him with. They repeated their accusations, in particular that by means of his teaching he was inciting unrest throughout the country from Galilee to Jerusalem. Then, recalling that they had said Galilee was the place where Jesus had begun teaching, Pilate inquired whether the man was indeed a Galilean. Learning that this was so, Pilate was pleased, for he thought he knew of a way that he might rid himself of this disagreeable business. As a Galilean, Jesus fell under the jurisdiction of Herod, the prince of that region. Pilate accordingly sent Jesus to Herod, who happened to be in Jerusalem for the feast. Herod was delighted at the prospect of meeting Jesus — something he had been wanting to do for a long time, because he had heard so much about him and hoped to see him do something extraordinary. He asked Jesus many questions, while the high priests and their associates kept making accusations. Jesus made no reply whatever. He remained calm even when Herod and his courtiers subjected him to all sorts of ridicule, dressing him up in a gown that symbolized princely dignity.

Since Herod did not know what to do with Jesus, whom he regarded more as an object of derision than as someone deserving punishment, he sent Jesus back to Pilate. (Pilate's attentiveness in respecting Herod's jurisdiction over Jesus as a Galilean had the effect of restoring a broken friendship between the two.) Pilate, perplexed as before, called the high priests and members of the Council together. He explained that although they had accused this individual of being a fomentor of unrest, he himself, like Herod, could not find any crime warranting a death penalty. There was nothing he could do beyond having him scourged, after which he would be set free. But the Jews were not satisfied with this punishment, and kept pressing for the death penalty.

Pilate, admiring Jesus' calm throughout these proceedings, was quite unwilling to be the instrument whereby he would be sacrificed to Jewish religious hatred, and, receiving encouragement from his wife, who had also taken an interest in Jesus, hit upon another expedient.
133 It was customary during Passover / for the Roman governor to grant a Jewish prisoner life and liberty. He knew of another Jew then in prison, Barabbas, whose people had charged him with numerous robberies and homicides. Hoping that the Jews would not want to dispense with this custom and would demand Jesus' freedom rather than that of a murderer, he left it up to them to choose between the two — between Barabbas and "the King of the Jews," as he mockingly referred to Jesus. But the priests easily persuaded the crowd to demand the release of Barabbas and the death of Jesus. When Pilate asked them what they had decided, which one he should set free, they shouted "Barabbas!" Exasperated, Pilate shouted back: "And what am I supposed to do with Jesus?" "Crucify him!" they screamed. "But what evil has he done?" Pilate asked once more. But they shouted, still more loudly: "To the cross, to the cross with him!" So Pilate then had Jesus scourged, and the soldiers braided him a crown of thorns (hogweed, *heracleum*), placed it on his head, dressed him in a purple robe, and put a stick instead of a scepter in his hand, shouting as they kicked him: "Hail, King of the Jews!" Hoping to find their fury satiated by all this, Pilate said to the Jews: "I repeat that I find nothing blameworthy in him." He ordered Jesus to be brought forth in this attire and said: "Behold him, feast your eyes on this spectacle." But it did not appease them; ever more stridently they demanded his death. "Then take him!" shouted Pilate, his patience wearing thin. "Crucify him! But I do not find him guilty!" The Jews responded: "By our laws he deserves capital punishment, for he has put himself forth as the Deity's own son." Pilate, who in keeping with Roman notions could only imagine a son of the gods, became still more hesitant, and asked Jesus: "Who are you really?" But Jesus gave no answer. "What!" said Pilate: "Now you will not answer even me? Do you know that your life and your death are entirely in my hands?" Jesus replied: "Only so far as my life and my death fit into the plan of divine providence. But this does not lessen the guilt of those who delivered me up to you."

Pilate found himself taking more of an interest in Jesus, and was inclined to set him free. The Jews, who sensed this, now threw themselves into the role of loyal subjects whose only concern was Caesar's well-being—a role they must have found difficult to play, but one that could hardly fail to further their cause. "If you set this one free," they shouted, "you are no friend of Caesar's; for anyone who professes to be a king is in rebellion against our emperor." Pilate thereupon presided over formal sentencing and had Jesus brought forward. "Behold your king! Shall I have your king nailed to a cross?" / "Crucify him! We recognize no king other than Caesar!" As the tumultuous uproar kept intensifying, Pilate had reason to fear disorder, perhaps even rebellion—one that could make the Jews appear zealous for the honor of Caesar while putting Pilate himself in an extremely dangerous position. Perceiving their obstinacy to be invincible, Pilate ordered a vessel to be filled with fresh water and, washing his hands in full view of the people, said: "I am innocent of the blood of this righteous individual. You shall have to answer for it!" The Jews cried: "Yes, let the punishment for his death be visited upon us and upon our children!"

134

The victory of the Jews was decisive: Barabbas was set free and Jesus was condemned to death on the cross (a Roman manner of execution as dishonorable as is death on the gallows today). Jesus remained exposed to the cruel mockery and abuse of the soldiers until he was led out to the place of execution. Ordinarily the condemned person had to drag out the cross-arm himself. But it was taken away from Jesus and a man named Simon, who was standing nearby, was made to carry it. The surging crowd was very large, and the friends of Jesus did not dare to come close, but followed behind in scattered fashion, observing the execution from a considerable distance. Closer to him were several women who had known him and were now weeping and wailing over his fate. Jesus turned to them as he walked and said: "Do not weep for me. You women of Jerusalem should rather weep for yourselves and your children. There are times ahead when the childless—when breasts that never gave suck, when women who never gave birth—will be deemed fortunate. You see what is happening to me; draw your own conclusion as to where such a spirit among a people may yet bring it."

Jesus was crucified in the company of two criminals, his cross having been set up between theirs. While he was being fastened to it (his hands were nailed to it, but his feet were probably only tied on),* Jesus cried out: "Father, forgive them, for they do not know what they are doing!" The soldiers divided up his clothing among themselves, as was the custom. Pilate had an inscription in Hebrew, Greek, and Latin attached above the cross: "This is the king of the Jews." This annoyed the priests, who were of the opinion that Pilate should have written only that Jesus had claimed to be the king of the Jews. But Pilate was still furious with them over the whole case, and was glad to see that the embarrassment intended by the inscription was not lost on them; and he replied to their requests that it be changed: "What I have written will remain."

135   Quite aside from the physical pain, / Jesus was subjected throughout to the triumphant mockery of the Jewish populace, genteel and common alike, as well as to the crude barbs of the Roman soldiers. Even one of the two criminals being crucified along with him was in no way moved to compassion by their shared fate; indeed this did not prevent him from adding his own scorn to that of the crowd. But the other had not become so completely alienated from human feeling and conscience in the course of his crimes. He reproached the former for continuing to be bitter in such circumstances and against someone who found himself in the same plight. "Besides," he added, "our fate is just, for we are receiving what our deeds deserved; whereas this one, though blameless, has been visited by a similar fortune!" Remember me," he said to Jesus, "when you are in your kingdom." "Soon the land of the blessed," Jesus replied, "will receive both of us together."

At the foot of the cross, in deep affliction, stood the mother of Jesus, along with several of her friends. John, alone among the intimate friends of Jesus, was with them, sharing their sorrow. Jesus caught sight of them together, and said to his mother: "There is your son in my stead," and to John: "Look upon her as your mother." In keeping with the wish of his dying friend, John did in fact take her into his house and care.

After hanging on the cross for several hours, Jesus, overcome by pain, cried out: "My God, my God, why have you abandoned me?" When he had called out that he was thirsty and had taken a little

---

Pauline Memorabilia. (1793), pp. 36–64: "An ancient problem regarding the nailing up of the feet among the crucified."

vinegar[5] from a sponge held up to him, he said: "It is completed."
And finally he cried out in a loud voice: "Father, into your hands
I commend my spirit." Then he bent his head and died.

Even the Roman centurion in charge of the execution admired the
quiet composure and unwavering dignity with which Jesus died. His
friends had watched the demise of their beloved teacher from afar.

Since as a rule the crucified perished slowly and often remained
alive on the mast for several days, and since the following day was
a major feast day, the Jews bade Pilate to have the legs of the condemned broken and to have them taken down so that their bodies
would not be on the cross in the morning. This was done to the
two criminals who had been sentenced with Jesus, for they were still
alive; but they saw that this was not necessary with Jesus, and so
merely stuck a spear in his side, from which / flowed water (lymph-   136
atic fluid) mixed with blood.

Joseph of Arimathea, who was a member of the High Council
in Jerusalem (it not being common knowledge that he was also a
friend of Jesus), begged Pilate to entrust Jesus' corpse to him. Pilate
allowed this; so together with Nicodemus, another friend, Joseph took
the dead one down from the cross, anointed him with myrrh and
aloe, wrapped him in linen, and buried him in his family's tomb,
which had been hewn into a rock in his garden. It being near the
place of execution, they were able to finish these services that much
sooner, before the beginning of the feast, during which it would not
have been permitted to deal with the dead.

5. In the margin of the page at this point: *legon aphete*—"now let him be, do
not tease him any further, lest he die too soon; it will only spoil our fun if Elias
comes and helps him." —Mark 15:36.

Selected Bibliography

There have been five comprehensive German editions of Hegel's collected works in this century. The most frequently cited is *Sämtliche Werke. Jubiläumsausgabe in zwanzig Bänden*. Edited by Hermann Glockner. Stuttgart: Fromanns, 1927–1930. Felix Meiner (Hamburg) has published two editions of Hegel's *Sämtliche Werke* —the first, published in the 1920s, under the editorship of Georg Lasson, and the second, a New Critical Edition published in the 1950s, under the editorship of Johannes Hoffmeister. Meiner's current edition of Hegel's *Gesammelte Werke* has been under way since 1968. Finally, Suhrkamp has published a (paperback) edition of Hegel's *Werke*, edited by Eva Moldenhauer and Karl Markus Michel. For a more extensive bibliography, see Kurt Steinhauer, *Hegel Bibliographie*. Munich: K. G. Sauer, 1980.

I. Works published by Hegel:

Differenz des Fichte'schen und Schelling'schen Systems der Philosophie (1801). In *Erste Druckschriften, Sämtliche Werke*, vol. 1. Edited by Georg Lasson. Leipzig: F. Meiner, 1928; *The Difference Between Fichte's and Schelling's Systems of Philosophy*. Translated by H. S. Harris and W. Cerf. Albany: SUNY Press, 1977.

"Glauben und Wissen." *Kritische Journal der Philosophie* 2, 1 (1802); *Faith and Knowledge*. Translated by W. Cerf and H. S. Harris. Albany: SUNY Press, 1977.

Phänomenologie des Geistes (1807). *Sämtliche Werke*, New Critical Edition, vol. 2. Hamburg: Felix Meiner, 1952; *The Phenomenology of Mind*. Translated by J. B. Baillie. New York: Harper and Row, 1967; *Hegel's Phenomenology of Spirit*. Translated by A. V. Miller. Oxford: Oxford University Press, 1979. For a translation of Hegel's essay-length "Preface" see W. Kaufmann, *Hegel: Texts and Commentary*. New York: Anchor, 1966 (reprinted Notre Dame, Ind.: University of Notre Dame Press, 1977).

Wissenschaft der Logik (1812–13). *Werke*, vols. 5–6. Frankfurt: Suhrkamp, 1972; *The Science of Logic*. 2 vols. Translated by W. H. Johnston and L. C. Struthers. London: Allen and Unwin, 1929; *Hegel's Science of Logic*. Translated by A. V. Miller. London: Allen and Unwin, 1969.

Enzyclopädie der philosophischen Wissenschaften im Grundrisse (1817, 1827, 1830), comprising the shorter Logic, the Philosophy of Nature, and the Philosophy of Spirit. *Werke*, vols. 8–10. Frankfurt: Suhrkamp, 1970; *The Logic of Hegel*. Translated by W. Wallace. Oxford: Clarendon, 1874; *Hegel's Philosophy of Nature*. Translated by A. V. Miller and W. Wallace. Oxford:

Clarendon, 1970; *Hegel's Philosophy of Mind.* Translated by A. V. Miller and W. Wallace. Oxford: Clarendon, 1971.

Grundlinien der Philosophie des Rechts (1821). *Sämtliche Werke,* New Critical Edition, vol. 12. Hamburg: Felix Meiner, 1955; *Hegel's Philosophy of Right.* Translated by T. M. Knox. London: Clarendon, 1952 (reprinted London: Oxford University Press, 1973).

"Uber die englische Reformbill." *Allgemeine Preussische Staatszeitung,* 1831. Translated by T. M. Knox in *Hegel's Political Writings.* Oxford: Clarendon, 1964.

II. Manuscripts, Lectures, etc. by Hegel, published posthumously:

Frühe Schriften. Werke, vol. 1. Frankfurt: Surhkamp, 1971.

Dokumente zu Hegels Entwicklung. Edited by J. Hoffmeister. Stuttgart: Frommanns, 1936.

Hegels theologische Jugendschriften. Edited by H. Nohl. Tübingen: J. C. B. Mohr, 1907; Selected English translations in *Early Theological Writings.* Translated by T. M. Knox. Chicago: University of Chicago Press, 1948 (reprinted New York: Harper Torchbooks, 1961).

Jenaer Schriften (1801–07). *Werke,* vol. 2. Frankfurt: Suhrkamp, 1970 (includes the published *Differenzschrift* and *Glauben und Wissen*).

Jenenser Realphilosophie (1803–06). Lectures on Philosophy of Nature and of Spirit. Edited by J. Hoffmeister. *Sämtliche Werke,* vols. 19–20. Leipzig: Felix Meiner, 1931–32.

System of Ethical Life and First Philosophy of Spirit. Translated by H. S. Harris and T. M. Knox. Albany: SUNY, 1979.

Schriften zur Politik und Rechtsphilosophie. Sämtliche Werke, vol. 7. Leipzig: Felix Meiner, 1913, 1923; Selections in *Hegel's Political Writings.* Edited by Z. Pelczynski. Oxford: Clarendon, 1964.

Berliner Schriften (1818–31). *Werke,* vol. 11. Frankfurt: Suhrkamp, 1970.

Vorlesungen über die Philosophie der Geschichte. Werke, vol. 12. Frankfurt: Suhrkamp, 1970; *The Philosophy of History.* Translated by J. Sibree. New York: Dover, 1956.

Vorlesungen über die Aesthetik. Werke, vols. 13–15. Frankfurt: Suhrkamp, 1970; *Hegel's Aesthetics: Lectures on Fine Art.* 2 vols. Translated by T. M. Knox. Oxford: Clarendon, 1975.

Vorlesungen über die Philosophie der Religion. Werke, vols. 16–17. Frankfurt: Suhrkamp, 1970; *Lectures on the Philosophy of Religion.* 3 vols. Translated by E. B. Spiers and J. B. Sanderson. London: K. Paul, Trench, Trübner & Co., 1895 (reprinted New York: Humanities Press, 1962).

Vorlesungen über die Geschichte der Philosophie. Werke, vols. 18–20. Frankfurt: Suhrkamp, 1970; *Lectures on the History of Philosophy.* 3 vols. Translated by E. S. Haldane and F. H. Simpson. London: K. Paul, Trench, Trübner & Co., 1892–96 (reprinted New York: Humanities Press, 1963).

Hegel's Philosophy of Subjective Spirit. 3 vols. Bilingual edition. Edited and translated by M. J. Petry. Boston: D. Reidel, 1978.

Briefe von und an Hegel. Sämtliche Werke, New Critical Edition, vols. 27–30. Hamburg: Felix Meiner, 1952. Chapter 7 of W. Kaufmann, *Hegel: A Reinterpretation.* Garden City, N.Y.: Doubleday, 1965 (reprinted Notre Dame, Ind.: University of Notre Dame Press, 1978) contains translations of selected correspondence.

III. Secondary Sources:

Asveld, Paul. *La pensée religieuse du jeune Hegel.* Louvain: Publications Universitaires, 1953.

Brecht, Martin and Jorg Sandberger. "Hegel's Begegnung mit der Theologie im Tübinger Stift." *Hegel-Studien* 5 (1969): 47–81.

Chapelle, Albert. *Hegel et la religion.* Paris: Editions Universitaires, 1963.

Christiansen, Darrel E., ed. *Hegel and the Philosophy of Religion.* The Hague: Martinus Nijhoff, 1970.

Dilthey, Wilhelm. *Die Jugendgeschichte Hegels* (1906). In *Gesammelte Schriften,* vol. 4. Stuttgart: B. G. Teubner, 1959.

Fackenheim, Emil. *The Religious Dimension in Hegel's Thought.* Bloomington: Indiana University Press, 1967.

Findlay, J. N. *Hegel: A Re-examination.* London: Allen and Unwin, 1958.

Glockner, Hermann. *Hegel.* 2 vols. Stuttgart: Frommanns, 1929.

Gorlend, Ingtraud. *Die Kantkritik des jungen Hegel.* Frankfurt: Vittorio Klostermann, 1966.

Gray, J. Glenn. *Hegel and Greek Thought.* New York: Harper, 1968.

Guerenu, Ernesto M. D. de. *Das Gottesbild des jungen Hegel.* Munich: Karl Alber, 1969.

Haering, Theodor. *Hegel: Sein Wollen und sein Werk.* 2 vols. Berlin: B. G. Teubner, 1929.

Harris, H. S. *Hegel's Development: Toward the Sunlight, 1770–1801.* Oxford: Clarendon Press, 1972.

Henrich, Dieter. *Hegel im Kontext.* Frankfurt: Suhrkamp, 1971.

Hoffmeister, Johannes. *Hölderlin und Hegel in Frankfurt.* Tübingen: J. C. B. Mohr, 1931.

Hölderlin, Johann Christian Friedrich. *Werke und Briefe.* Edited by F. Beissner and J. Schmidt. 3 vols. Frankfurt: Insel, 1969.

Hyppolite, Jean. *Genesis and Structure of Hegel's Phenomenology of Spirit* (1946). Translated by S. Cherniak and J. Heckman. Evanston: Northwestern University Press, 1974.

Kant, Immanuel. *Critique of Pure Reason.* Translated by N. K. Smith. New York: St. Martin's Press, 1965.

————. *Critique of Practical Reason.* Translated and edited by L. W. Beck. Indianapolis: Bobbs-Merrill, 1956.

————. *Foundations of the Metaphysics of Morals* and *What is Enlightenment?* Translated by L. W. Beck. Indianapolis: Bobbs-Merrill, 1959.

————. *Religion within the Limits of Reason Alone.* Translated by T. M. Greene and H. H. Hudson. New York: Harper and Row, 1960.

Kaufmann, Walter. "Hegel's Early Antitheological Phase." *Philosophical Review* 63 (1954): 3–18.

————. *Hegel: A Reinterpretation.* Garden City, N.Y.: Doubleday, 1965 (reprint Notre Dame, Ind.: University of Notre Dame Press, 1978).

————. *Hegel: Texts and Commentary.* New York: Anchor Books, 1966 (reprint Notre Dame, Ind.: University of Notre Dame Press, 1977).

Kelly, George A. *Idealism, Politics and History: Sources of Hegelian Thought.* Cambridge: Cambridge University Press, 1969.

Klaiber, Julius. *Hölderlin, Hegel und Schelling in ihren schwäbischen Jugendjahren.* Stuttgart: J. G. Cotta, 1877.

Knox, T. M. "Hegel's Attitude to Kant's Ethics." *Kant-Studien* 49 (1957–8): 70–81.

Kojève, Alexandre. *Introduction to the Reading of Hegel* (1947). Edited by A. Bloom. Translated by J. H. Nichols. New York: Basic Books, 1969.

Kroner, Richard. *Von Kant bis Hegel* (1921, 1924). 2 vols. Tübingen: J. C. B. Mohr, 1961.

Kruger, Hans-Joachim. *Theologie und Aufklärung: Untersuchungen zu ihrer Vermittlung beim jungen Hegel.* Stuttgart: J. B. Metzlersche, 1966.

Lacorte, Carmelo. *Il primo Hegel.* Florence: Sansoni, 1959.

Lauer, Quentin. *Hegel's Concept of God.* Albany: SUNY Press, 1982.

Lessing, Gotthold Ephraim. *Laocoon, Nathan the Wise, Minna von Barnhelm.* Translated by W. A. Steel and A. Dent. London: Dent (Everyman), 1930.

————. *Theological Writings.* Translated by H. Chadwick. London: A. and C. Black, 1956.

Löwith, Karl. "Hegels Aufhebung der christlichen Religion." *Hegel-Studien* 1 (1962): 193–236.

Lukács, Gyorgy. *The Young Hegel* (1948). Translated by R. Livingstone. Cambridge: M.I.T. Press, 1976 (especially chapter one).

Mueller, Gustav Emil. *Hegel: The Man, His Vision and Work.* New York: Pageant Press, 1968.

Mure, G. R. G. *An Introduction to Hegel.* Oxford: Clarendon Press, 1940.

————. *The Philosophy of Hegel.* London: Oxford University Press, 1965.

————. "Hegel, Luther, and the Owl of Minerva." *Philosophy* 41 (1966): 127–139.

Peperzak, A. T. B. *Le jeune Hegel et la vision morale du monde*. The Hague: Martinus Nijhoff, 1969.

———. "Existenz und Denken im Werden der Hegelschen Philosophie." *Scholastik* 38 (1963): 226–238.

Pfleiderer, Otto. *The Development of Theology in Germany since Kant*. Translated by J. F. Smith. London: Sonnenschein, 1893.

Rebstock, Hans-Otto. *Hegels Auffassung des Mythos in seinen Frühschriften*. Freiburg: K. Alber, 1971.

Ritter, Joachim. *Hegel und die französische Revolution*. Köln: Westdeutscher Verlag, 1957.

Rohrmoser, Gunther. "Zur Vorgeschichte der Jugendschriften Hegels." *Zeitschrift für philosophische Forschung* 14 (1960): 182–208.

———. *Theologie et Aliénation dans la pensée du jeune Hegel*. Paris: Beauchesne, 1970.

Rosen, Stanley. *G. W. F. Hegel: An Introduction to the Science of Wisdom*. New Haven: Yale University Press, 1974.

Rosenzweig, Franz. *Hegel und der Staat*. 2 vols. Munich: R. Oldenbourg, 1920 (reprinted Aalen: Scientia, 1962).

Schelling, Friedrich Wilhelm Joseph. *Sämmtliche Werke*. 14 vols. Stuttgart: Cotta, 1856–61 (selectively reprinted Darmstadt: Wissenschaftliche Buchgesellschaft, 1974–76).

Schüler, Gisela. "Zur Chronologie von Hegels Jugendschriften." *Hegel-Studien* 2 (1963): 111–159.

Splett, Jorg. *Die Trinitätslehre G. W. F. Hegels*. Munich: Karl Alber, 1965.

Strahm, Hans. "Aus Hegels Berner Zeit." *Archiv für Geschichte der Philosophie* 41 (1932): 514–33.

Steinkraus, Warren E., ed. *New Studies in Hegel's Philosophy*. New York: Holt, Rinehart and Winston, 1971.

Taylor, Charles. *Hegel*. Cambridge: Cambridge University Press, 1975.

White, Alan. *Schelling: An Introduction to the System of Freedom*. New Haven: Yale University Press, 1983.

Yerkes, James. *The Christology of Hegel*. Albany: SUNY Press, 1983.

IV. Biographies:

Caird, Edward. *Hegel*. Edinburgh: W. Blackwood & Sons, 1883 (reprinted New York: AMS Press, 1972).

Haym, Rudolf. *Hegel und seine Zeit*. Berlin: Gaertner, 1857 (reprinted Hildesheim: Georg Olms, 1962).

Rosenkranz, Karl. *Hegels Leben*. Berlin: Deucker und Humblot, 1844.

Wiedmann, Franz. *Hegel: An Illustrated Biography*. Translated by J. Neugroschel. New York: Pegasus, 1968.

Index

Abraham: 105, 140
Adam: 25
Aesculapius: 63f
Agathon: 56
Ananias: 71
Andrew (the Apostle): 110
Apollo: 82
Apostles: 17, 61f, 90, 107, 123
Augustine: 25
Authority: 49, 98, 118

Bacchus: 85f
Barabbas: 162
Baucis: 66
Beatitudes: 110f
Brahma: 136

Caesar: 149, 163
Caiaphas: 158
Campe, J. H. (*Theophron*): 40, 43
Christ: alienation from his own
  people, 14; death of, 28, 91; as
  divine, 89, 101; as embodiment
  of virtue, 62, 68, 89, 99, 104;
  historical actuality of, 96f;
  moral emulation of, 71, 88f;
  resurrection of, 29; three temptations of, 106
Christian: afterlife, 10, 12, 22,
  76, 86f; alienation, 2, 56, 68,
  72f, 80; attitude toward death,
  76f; baptism, 53; conceptual
  truth, 19, 21; depravity, 95,
  101f; divine justice, 26, 97;
  ecclesiastical discipline, 72–74;
  eucharist, 53; grace, 23, 97;
  incarnation, 7, 22, 25, 27;
  irrational or mysterious doctrines, 11f, 30–33, 70, 81f, 83f;
  Original Sin, 12, 25, 90; other-

Christian (*continued*)
  worldliness, 70f; political activity, 9, 13, 27–29, 69f, 72f,
  97f; propitiation, 5, 90; providence, 50f, 89f; psychological
  demoralization, 72–74, 85, 87;
  resurrection, 64, 86; sacrifice,
  53; salvation, 12, 91; trinity,
  27, 90
Civic humanism: 22
Chronos (Time): 56n
Conscience: 37, 72f, 81, 127
Coriolanus: 38
Crusades: 69

Dante: 7, 24
David: 104, 119
Death: 76–78
Diogenes: 7, 60f
Diotima: 59

Education, moral and religious:
  35, 52, 59f, 75f, 97
Empiricism: 47
Enlightenment: 4, 8, 10, 39ff

Fichte: 23
Folk religion (cf. religion): 3, 9,
  12f, 32, 42, 49, 54f, 81, 98;
  criteria of, 5, 11, 33, 45, 49f,
  52f, 55f
Frederick II: 39, 67
Freedom: 1, 5, 12f, 22, 56, 63,
  69–74, 81, 95, 98
Freud: 8

Garden of Eden: 25
Gellert, Christian F.: 39
Goethe, J. W. v.: 127n
Good Samaritan: 132